THE CRISIS OF IDENTITY

The American of today lives in a world he never made. Isolated, lonely, cut off from the comforts of family and faith, this mobile citizen seeks to maintain identity in any way he can. Too often this way is through pseudo-politics, how-to religion, in-group membership, corporation teamship, PTA and Rotary meetings— anything that gives him the protective coloration of the crowd. Too seldom, according to an eminent European scientist, it is through an honest assessment of reality and a private evaluation of self.

As a psychoanalyst and sociologist, Dr. Ruitenbeek is able to view the American malady with scientific objectivity. His book is a valuable study of a little-understood subject: the loss of identity in a swiftly changing society . . . the plight of the new man who has not yet found his name or his place in a new world.

MENTOR Books of Related Interest

The
INDIVIDUAL
and the Crowd

A Study of Identity in America

Hendrik M. Ruitenbeek

MENTOR

A MENTOR BOOK
Published by
THE NEW AMERICAN LIBRARY,
New York and Toronto
The New English Library Limited, London

MENTOR TRADEMARK REG. U.S. PAT. OFF. AND FOREIGN COUNTRIES
REGISTERED TRADEMARK—MARCA REGISTRADA
HECHO EN CHICAGO, U.S.A.

MENTOR BOOKS are published *in the United States* by
The New American Library, Inc.,
1301 Avenue of the Americas, New York, New York 10019,
in Canada by The New American Library of Canada Limited,
295 King Street East, Toronto 2, Ontario,
in the United Kingdom by The New English Library Limited,
Barnard's Inn, Holborn, London, E.C. 1, England

FIRST PRINTING, MARCH, 1965

PRINTED IN THE UNITED STATES OF AMERICA

For Richard McConchie

Amicus est tanquam alter idem

"*At the beginning, identity is a dream.*

At the end, it is a nightmare."

—Larry Rivers and Frank O'Hara, in
"How to proceed in the arts"

ACKNOWLEDGMENTS

I would like to express my gratitude to all those who have assisted me in the preparation of this study. I am especially grateful to Mrs. Nobuyuki Siraisi who, in the early stages of writing this book, was most helpful in editing my first efforts; to Dr. Helene Zahler whose advice and editing of the finished manuscript, in particular her contributions to Chapter II, were invaluable; to Mr. Truman Talley of the New American Library of World Literature, Inc., who saw the first drafts of the manuscript and encouraged me to continue; to Miss Muriel Fleischman who painstakingly typed the manuscript; and finally to all my friends who have patiently listened to my monologues on problems of identity throughout the past years.

Hendrik M. Ruitenbeek

New York

January 1964

CONTENTS

Introduction 9

I The Problem of Identity 15

II Identity in History 31

III Existence and Identity 53

IV Psychoanalysis and Identity 63

V Character and Identity 72

VI Class and Identity 86

VII Anomie and Identity 93

VIII Identity in America 110

Bibliography 119

INTRODUCTION

This book is the result of a long-standing interest in the complex problems of American sociology. As a European student of the subject, I had been struck by the wide range of issues with which American scholars had dealt and by the dynamic and complex society that their studies revealed.[1] After my arrival in this country some eight years ago, my interest in social character and personality in America was particularly stimulated by the work of Erich Fromm and David Riesman,[2] who make the relationship between the individual's personality and his social character their particular concern. Personality I define with Edward Sapir as the totality of those aspects of behavior which give meaning to an individual in society and differentiate him from other members in the community. Social character, as Fromm and Riesman discuss it, is that aspect of the individual's "character" (the relatively stable pattern of behavior he shows in his actions and relationships) which he shares with members of his age group, his sex, his professional or occupational class, his ownership status, his nation, even his culture as a whole.[3]

In a swiftly changing technological society, the relationship between the individual's personal and social character generates many tensions. These tensions, in my opinion, give rise to the problems which afflict and, in a sense, create modern man. Hence, exploring this relationship helps us understand those problems. Investigation of those problems has not been lacking, of course. Many significant studies, sociological, religious, psychoanalytic, have explored the situation of man in contemporary America.[4] Other studies have approached

[1] For a current review of American sociology, consult Robert Merton, *et al.*, *Sociology Today* (New York, Basic Books, 1959), but remember that even this book does not give full coverage of all contemporary trends.

[2] David Riesman, *The Lonely Crowd* (New York, Doubleday Anchor).

[3] Erich Fromm, *Escape from Freedom* (New York, Rinehart and Co., 1941); *The Sane Society* (New York, Rinehart and Co., 1955); Riesman, *Lonely Crowd*, pp. 26-53.

[4] Hannah Arendt, *The Human Condition* (New York, Doubleday Anchor edition, 1959), uses a politico-sociological emphasis; Erich Kahler, *The Tower and the Abyss* (New York, George Braziller, 1957), is philosophically oriented; William H. Whyte, Jr., *The Organization Man* (New York, Doubleday Anchor, 1958), analyzes the influence of

that situation in more general and philosophical terms. The existentialists particularly—Gabriel Marcel, Karl Jaspers, Martin Heidegger, and Martin Buber—have given us broad yet penetrating accounts of the present condition of man.

The sociologists and psychologists have explored current dilemmas in terms of insecurity, alienation, anxiety, and social disorganization. The philosophers have seen current dilemmas as part of man's effort to live in and comprehend the universe. Yet neither the studies of the social scientists nor the speculations of the philosophers give us the common denominator needed for adequate understanding of the plight of man in a technological society. Such a common denominator is not easy to find, for the problem is many-faceted; no single discipline can define and interpret it completely. Yet if the social sciences are even to begin to move toward comprehension of their material, they must have some central concept around which scholars can orient their thinking. To my mind, identity appears to be such a concept.

For most social scientists, the concept of identity still has a specifically psychoanalytic reference and background. In *Childhood and Society,* Erik Erikson, for instance, uses "identity" to designate "the continuing I." He prefers *identity* to *self* or *ego,* for example, because it conveys the idea of a two-way process. *Identity* includes the relationship of oneself to oneself, of oneself to others, and of oneself to social institutions. Identity thus implies a continuity within the person and a continuous sharing of some essential character with other persons.

If we interpret the foregoing concept of identity culturally as well as psychoanalytically, as I propose to do, we may have a better key to the understanding of man's role in his social environment, especially as that exists today. The key is not magic, of course; identity is not the final word, the great sun about which all the planets of sociological and psychological study should revolve, but it may be useful.

Both my study of social scientists' work and my observa-

large-scale private organization on man in American society; Helen Merrell Lynd, *On Shame and the Search for Identity* (New York, Harcourt, Brace, and Co., 1958), approaches identity in terms of shame and guilt; Norman O. Brown, *Life Against Death* (New York, Random House, 1960), is a brilliant study of the relationship between psychoanalysis and history; Paul Tillich, *The Courage to Be* (New Haven, Yale University Press, 1952), studies contemporary anxiety from a theological point of view; Allen Wheelis, *The Quest for Identity* (New York, Norton, 1958), studies identity in contemporary society psychoanalytically; Herbert Marcuse, *Eros and Civilization* (Boston, Beacon Press, 1955), restates Freudian theory in terms of the problems of contemporary civilizations and argues its superiority to the neo-Freudian approach.

tion of the American scene from the vantage point of the European who does not take that scene for granted, as the born American very often does, lead me to conclude that American students of society have underestimated the potential usefulness of the identity concept. They have also tended to overlook the presence of an identity problem in America and to neglect issues centering around disturbance in the individual's sense of identity.

Broadly understood then, identity involves the individual as he exists in his society. Man must know who he is: he must be able to sense himself as both author and object of his actions. For the only true fulfillment of his human needs is his development as a fully individuated personality, which recognizes itself as the center of its own being. Such a personality has achieved identity. But that identity grows out of the interplay of many factors, many aspects of experience. Some of these factors are sociological, and it is those which are emphasized here. Others are psychological, and these are generally interpreted from a modified psychoanalytical point of view. Still other factors entering into the development of identity are philosophical, and those are dealt with in terms of the existential outlook, the belief that the basic problem with which man must contend is his existence; he is present in the world and must decide for himself how he shall live there. The sociological, psychological, and philosophical factors that enter into our understanding of the growth of identity change in time and the nature of identity changes with them; hence, these factors must also be seen historically.

This study is the outcome of a long search for a societal interpretation of the problems of individual existence in a mass society. Through its use of the concept of identity, this book may help sociologists achieve a more unified approach to the separate problems that occupy them. But since this is not primarily a book for specialists, I hope the reader may get some fresh insight into his own situation as a person in "a world he never made" and yet is always making.

Chapter I discusses the problem of identity in the United States. The problem is not exclusively American; it has long existed in Western Europe, too, as the work of European philosophers shows. But because society changes more slowly in Western Europe than in America, the problem is less acute there. The American scene presents the issues more sharply. Americans are said to be a relatively traditionless people. The tradition they do have, however, has tended to produce a cast of mind which, when it is aware of anything beyond external necessities, is likely to be self-examining. The American intellectual often seems to be an invisible audience watching the performance that is his life with a puzzled eye. When the nonintellectual American acts as his own audience, that audience tends to look to others for its cue to clap or boo. In both instances, the outside observer is aware of a concern for appearances and external evaluations that testifies to a rather fluctuating sense of identity.

Chapter II describes the American individual as he experiences the *identity crisis,* the search for that stable inner continuity that will help him exist more fully and independently than by mere identification with occupation, religion, or nation. Chapter III deals with identity problems of crucial periods in the past in order to achieve greater understanding of contemporary identity situations. It is sometimes assumed that identity crises are something altogether new. Only the felt acuteness is novel, however, the problem has always been present. Its medieval, Renaissance, Reformation, and nineteenth-century shapes are surveyed, for a single chapter can survey only; full presentation would require not one book but several shelves full.

Chapter IV deals with some philosophical implications of identity and the identity problem. Linking the idea of the self with the concept of identity is an exciting and original contemporary development, for the "self" of the nineteenth-century philosophers is completely different from the concept of identity developed by twentieth-century sociologists and psychoanalysts. There is, however, a subtle relationship between identity and the concept of "existence" developed by the existentialist philosophers. For these thinkers, the phenomena of despair, anxiety, and loneliness are extremely important; a like emphasis appears in the writings of social scientists concerned with the fate of the individual man in his mass society. Paul Tillich, theologian and philosopher, approaches the fate of man from a rather similar viewpoint and offers an existentialist interpretation of man's religious life in present society.

Chapter V discusses the emergence and significance of existential psychoanalysis, a subject that is currently arousing much interest among American psychologists and sociologists.[5] And one may well say that the appeal of existentialism and existential psychoanalysis for philosophers, literary men, and psychotherapists in the United States is itself linked with the identity crisis in modern America. Chapter V is thus closely

[5] See, particularly, Rollo May and Henri F. Ellenberger (eds.), *Existence* (New York, Basic Books, 1959); Kurt F. Reinhardt, *The Existentialist Revolt* (New York, Atlantic Paperbacks, 1960), p. 244; and Hendrik M. Ruitenbeek (ed.), *Psychoanalysis and Existential Philosophy* (New York, E. P. Dutton, 1962).

linked to Chapter IV. So far, there has been no substantial investigation into the impact of Freud's ideas on American society, and this is not an inquiry that can be undertaken within the compass of this rather short book. It does seem, however, that the underlying reasons for the wide appeal of Freud in the United States can be interpreted in terms of the American social structure. That structure, as will be shown, does not give full support to the development of identity. Contemporary American awareness of and receptivity to psychoanalytic thinking therefore is closely related to experience of the identity crisis.

Chapters VI through VIII deal with the problem of identity in more strictly sociological terms. Chapter VI defines and examines the American social character; Chapter VII explores identity in terms of some of the social conflicts that characterize our society. The growth of juvenile delinquency and adult crime illustrates social disorganization; the presence of and attitudes toward deviant behavior illustrate changing concepts of right and wrong, particularly in regard to sexual relationships. In our society, at least, deviant behavior is explicable as an aspect of a broader identity problem. Chapter VIII discusses in more detail the relationship between identity and the social structure both in terms of social theory[6] and in terms of the effect of mass culture in producing the current identity crisis in America. Closely linked with this, the final chapter discusses the future of identity, the fate of that continuous integrated core that makes a person feel real to himself and seem real (even if eccentric at times) to others. Chapter IX reaches no definitive conclusions, since I am a scholar, not a prophet, but it does present some issues and raise some questions that Americans must face both one by one, as individuals, and together, as the groups in which individuals find themselves and function.

This book is one of the first general studies of identity to be published; it does not claim to be comprehensive. For example, political identity, although it is extremely significant for an understanding of American life, is scarcely touched on. There is, however, an effort to survey in some depth the

[6] Here I refer to the works of Riesman, Fromm, Whyte, Tillich, and Wheelis previously cited. The reader may also consult the following anthologies, which show some major current trends in the study of man in mass society: Maurice Stein, Arthur J. Vidich, and David Manning White (eds.), *Identity and Anxiety: Survival of the Person in Mass Society* (New York, The Free Press of Glencoe, 1960); Bernard Rosenberg and D. M. White, *Mass Culture* (New York, The Free Press of Glencoe, 1957); Eric Larrabee and Rolf Meyersohn, *Mass Leisure* (New York, The Free Press of Glencoe, 1958).

sociological, philosophical, and psychoanalytic aspects of the concept of identity and the identity problem.

To close on a personal note, this book has emerged from my own deep concern about the importance and relevance of man as an individual in our particular society, technologically oriented, mechanized, shaped by and shaping a mass culture. Such a society has developed most rapidly and perhaps most fully in the United States. Both as observer and participant, I have become thoroughly involved with the sociological, philosophical, and psychological problems of the American people. My discussion here will, I hope, serve sociologists, philosophers, and psychologists; also, and more importantly, I hope this discussion will have meaning and usefulness for all those who are aware of the idea of identity or who feel that their own sense of identity is associated with personal, even anxiety-evoking problems.

I. THE PROBLEM OF IDENTITY

"Who am I?" "Where am I going?" "Do I belong?": these are the crucial questions man asks himself in modern mass society. And in these questions, the social scientist sees many of his scholarly concerns: adjustment, goal-direction, and role-playing, for example.

"Who am I?" stands for the person's need to know and to feel himself both as part of a larger social context and as a separate and unique being. The individual needs to differentiate himself, to be different from, and more than, the many aspects of living through which he establishes identification. The individual also needs to identify himself with a pattern of ideology, religion, occupation, and personal relationships (what the existentialists have called his Being-in-the-world). And to achieve identity, he needs to integrate separateness with sharing, the uniquely individual with the common (if we may play with words, the being a part with the being apart).

"Where am I going?" is a more specific sort of question. It involves a man's ability to direct his life, to set his goals, short term and long term. "Do I belong?" is still more specific, for if honestly faced, it requires a man to look at his personal and social environment, his family, his work, his school, his friends—and asks whether he belongs. Is he accepted here? Does he genuinely want to be accepted here?

Sociologists such as Robert Merton have discussed the impact of inability to achieve goals upon social behavior (see his book *Social Theory and Social Structure*[1]). On another level, such a perceptive journalist as William H. Whyte, Jr.[2] has sketched the plight of the person whose livelihood depends on his ability to convince other people and himself that he is where he belongs and that he belongs where he is.

Thus, the three questions with which this chapter begins have far-reaching and challenging implications, philosophical, sociological, and psychoanalytic. These questions sum up some crucial problems of man in our time, problems that are best understood in terms of the concept of identity and the crisis through which identity is passing.

[1] New York: The Free Press of Glencoe, rev. ed., 1957.
[2] *The Organization Man* (New York: Doubleday Anchor Books, 1957).

Today, individuals frequently encounter difficulties in relating themselves to their environment and to society in general. Their attempt to relate themselves to society is expressed in the choices and decisions they make, yet these very choices and decisions are often the source of their difficulty in identifying themselves with the society that requires those choices to be made. Thus, the roots of the problem of individual identity in our society are to be found in the intricate relationships of self and environment and of self and society. Since these relationships dictate both the individual's personal and his *cultural identity*, it is obvious that any significant breakdown in these relationships will produce an identity crisis. This crisis is not merely *individual*, for it is not peculiar to the person undergoing it: rather the modern identity crisis is shared with others who find themselves in a similar position *vis à vis* society.

From a psychological and psychoanalytical viewpoint, Freud's findings on the roles of the superego, the ego, and the id are extremely important for understanding the problem of identity.[3] Everyone knows that the *id* is the reservoir of instinctual energies; the *superego* is the commands and prohibitions of the parents (and, through them, of the society), which the child incorporates into itself; and the *ego* is the means by which the person orients himself toward reality. The personality develops as a result of the interaction between id, ego, and superego. Changes in any one of the three will produce changes in the relationship among them and so will affect both the personality and the identity of the individual. In the personality as Freud encountered and described it, the superego played a dominating, indeed often a domineering role. The nineteenth century saw itself as an age of disintegrating values, but to us it seems an age of stability. So, until World War I, father really did know best; the wisdom of age seemed relevant, and customary ways of behaving and believing had authority. Since 1919, and particularly in the United States, rapid change has become the rule. Age no longer even appears wise (except perhaps in Germany where youth had its day with Hitler), and the authority of custom tends to diminish. Within the family, parental authority grows weaker. But authority in the family has been eroded during the course of a long historical process, which has undermined many of the shared ideals that society has cherished and wished to perpetuate. Thus, what may be called the *social* superego has lost authority at the very time that the character

---

[3] See particularly Sigmund Freud's *Civilization and Its Discontents* (New York: Doubleday Anchor Books, 1958) and *The Future of an Illusion* (New York: Doubleday Anchor Books, 1957).

of the family has been changing. The contemporary psycho-therapist rarely sees in his patients the dominating superego, which Freud portrayed. The superego's role in forming individual identity has tended to decline.

The ego, lacking specific direction from the superego, tends to reflect the instability and insecurity of contemporary man and his society. Often the ego cannot give adequate direction to the person, and identity is weak. As a result of the declining superego and an insecure ego, the forces of the id are closer to the surface in the contemporary personality. In this way, identity may be undermined because neither ego nor superego can be confident of control of the id forces. Today, the individual may be more immediately confronted by the id than he has been since the medieval period.

With ego and superego control over the id thus undermined and with the stability of social values seriously weakened, the individual faces identity problems on many levels. The loss of stable values makes the development of the superego more hazardous. Individuals can no longer fall back upon established values; they must look for other ways to feel secure and thus to identify themselves with their environment and with society. But, in large measure, the authority of values depends upon their being taken for granted. It is extremely difficult to replace one set of values with another. When a man loses his faith, that is, the values upon which he has relied, he feels insecure, unrelated, and *unidentified*. He may be able to establish a new identification, but that often requires fairly rigorous intellectual activity. In a changing, dynamic society, like that of America today, it is easier to lose values than it is in a comparatively static environment. And it is much more difficult to build new values. As we shall see in Chapter II, the individual found it easier to identify himself with his environment in societies that emphasized the preservation of tradition; he had identity problems then, too, but they were of a different kind.

A superego deprived of reinforcement from without cannot make a full contribution to the development of identity through identification. The ego, on the other hand, is confronted by a peculiarly demanding reality, which is presented by the culture of our time. And so far as we know, id forces have lost none of their energy.

In situations involving stress, therefore, and stress is built into contemporary life, the individual is likely to experience some form of identity crisis. Certain stress situations, of course, may be considered part of the "natural history" of man. Primitive people have developed elaborate rituals to mark some of these, the great human experiences: birth, the appearance of sexual maturity, death. Modern society has its rites, of course, and some of them may channel stress situations in ways that make them manageable. More generally, however, modern men must face their stresses as individuals. Often, critical situations in the personal environment, the need to modify or develop a significant personal relationship, for example, may give rise to an identity crisis.

Persons affected by such a crisis cease to feel that their endeavors, and their lives in general, "make sense": the values that have seemed stable cease to be dependable. The person often becomes unable to decide what is right for him in a situation. He has moral convictions, say, and a family to support. Is it right for him to put his moral welfare, his integrity, before his social obligations? Thus the individual faces an identity crisis because he can no longer make the choice which, he thinks, society demands of him and still retain his feeling of being true to himself. If this inability to make choices becomes habitual, then the individual is forced into a pattern of life essentially without meaning. His total existence is of such a kind that he cannot identify himself either in or with it. This is a personal existential tragedy, but it has wider implications, confronting us with the general existential situation of modern man, lost in the web of choices and decisions that society demands of him.

As far as our discussion is concerned, the consequences for the man who cannot face making the choices required by society are even more significant, for the problem of identity arises precisely when the individual is caught in an unresolved existential situation. In such a situation, a man is no longer master of himself or of his circumstances. Attribution of stable values and confusion in concepts of personal right and wrong may well arise and produce personal insecurity, anxiety, and what may be termed societal anomie. Anxiety and insecurity are specific individual experiences, but they cannot be separated from the sufferer's relationship with his environment and, more particularly, with his family, friends, and business associates. Anxiety and insecurity can develop in any of these relationships in response to a breakdown of the relationship between self and environment or self and society. Societal anomie, not being dependent on a particular individual experience, is more likely to develop in connection with identity crises determined by the relationship with society. One may, therefore, distinguish individual identity crises and identity crises that exist in societal organizations and institutions. The personal and the group identity crises are closely related and it is impossible to treat them separately.

A number of psychoanalysts and philosophers have dealt

with the problem of personal identity. In *The Quest for Identity* Allen Wheelis suggests that the twentieth-century development of psychoanalysis is not merely the story of the growth of a self-sufficient discipline, but rather illustrates how particular characteristics in our Western society have fostered its development. Wheelis, like Erik Erikson, considers the personal identity crisis in the larger context, that is, the half-century social change that has affected the roles and the behavior of individuals in our society. For we must continue to emphasize the close relationship between identity crises as experienced by the individual and the problem of identity in its social context. In *Childhood and Society,* for example, Erik Erikson describes the identity crisis in terms of the experiences of adolescents and speaks of the "major crisis of adolescence" in our time. He thus approaches adolescence in terms of *Sturm und Drang,* as defined by philosophers and poets,[4] incidentally, long before either sociology or psychology was a recognized intellectual discipline. Erikson further develops the concept of the identity crisis in *Young Man Luther,* where he treats Luther's youth and young maturity in these terms. He endeavors to associate Luther's individual crisis with the major identity crisis in the society of his time and says:

> This calls for an investigation of how the individual "case" became an important, and historic "event," and for formulations concerning the spiritual and political crisis of Northern Christendom in Luther's time. . . . We clinicians have learned in recent years that we cannot lift a case out of history, even as we suspect that historians, when they try to separate the logic of the historic event from that of the life histories which intersect in it, leave a number of vital historical problems unattended.[5]

Erikson thus emphasizes the spiritual and political crisis, which colored Luther's social environment. We, too, may inquire what impact such social stress, if it exists, may have upon the identity crisis of our time. Currently, we are in the midst of a spiritual crisis, as the emergence of a new dialectical theology illustrates. The influence of Karl Barth and Paul Tillich shows how thin is the line between philosophy and theology and how close are the crises in those areas of human

---

[4] A classic literary illustration of a *Sturm und Drang* period is Goethe's *Das Leiden des Jungen Werthers* (*The Sufferings of Young Werther*).

[5] Erik H. Erikson, *Young Man Luther* (New York: W. W. Norton & Co., Inc., 1958), pp. 15-16.

concern. Another theologian, Reinhold Niebuhr, all but personifies the contemporary crisis in liberal politics, where technological developments tend to make political institutions obsolete and political ideologies irrelevant. The crisis in "morals" is illustrated by the social strains and the social problems of which we are all too aware: delinquency, crime, deviant sexual behavior, family disintegration, insecurity, alienation.

Similar indications of social disorganization have been evident in the past, of course. Men have experienced widespread identity crises before. What characterizes our time is the more acute impact of events upon persons who are often more psychologically and even sociologically sophisticated, and hence more aware of discomfort, whether that be social or personal. Yet, at the same time, we should distinguish between the concern of the educated and particularly the professionals, whether they be social scientists, theologians, or journalists, and the acquiescence of the majority. Most persons continue to accept their social world with complacency. They do not worry about disquieting trends unless they are specifically pointed or unless they make themselves painfully evident. Even then, those who suffer do not usually understand the particular societal situation that has resulted in crisis for them.

Increasingly, however, although often in rather shallow terms, even the acquiescent majority is learning something about the nature of their time and some of its characteristic afflictions. Social scientists can make a major contribution to society's well-being by investigating the varied identity crises of our time in terms of the questions "Who am I?" and "Do I belong?" and by emphasizing the significance of a proper understanding of one's own identity if the person is to function harmoniously both as an individual and in relation to society. (And it may be hoped that the social scientists will make their inquiries fruitful by learning how to talk to the public as well as to each other.)

Currently, sociologists and psychoanalytically oriented social psychologists are studying many aspects of the present crisis. Their research has given us much information, often in highly refined statistical form, in such areas as class conflict, the behavior of small groups, the nature and content of public opinion, and the like. But many American sociologists are interested in their own specialties; they devote their effort to specific social research and tend to neglect general sociological ideas.[6] David Riesman and Ernest van den Haag are

6 Sociologists, such as Seymour Lipset, Reinhard Bendix, Robert Merton, Talcott Parsons, Paul Lazarsfeld, have contributed significant

Role-playing/ Roles

notable exceptions, of course. On the whole, however, academic sociologists either ignore the need for developing frames of reference which will give their detailed research background and real meaning or they cast their theories in such vague and pretentious language that the whole enterprise of sociological generalization tends to be discredited.

Sociology and social psychology are supposed to concern themselves with the problems of man in society, yet the concentration of American sociologists on their narrow fields of specialization has encouraged them to turn the distresses of the individual to the psychotherapist and the problems of society to society itself. Most social scientists have been working only on the fringes of the issues that confront the individual in society. Although significant psychoanalytic and sociological studies do present research data on the problems of the individual in his environment and in society, they generally consider the context of these problems in a severely limited way. In many cases, the writers are so involved in observing the incidentals of the problem, that they never become able to construct the framework necessary for even a beginning of general interpretation.

As a result, the distresses of our time are studied separately rather than in the context of a coherent frame of reference. In exploring some aspects of the concept of identity, individual and societal, it may be possible to take at least some preliminary steps toward the building of such a framework. We have described how the individual develops his identity through his experience with parents, with his peers, with superiors, with the physical and social world about him. As an outcome of this total experience, the person establishes his identity in both its phases, identification with and separateness from, the social environment. To a great extent, role-playing provides the link between individual and social identity. The person acts certain roles, which give him meaning and distinction as an individual in society. At the same time these roles are essential for his functioning as a part of society; thus they form the bridge between his individual identity and the social identity. Useful as the role-playing concept is, and familiar as most sociologists are with it, too many of them have failed to effect a satisfactory correlation of the concepts of role-playing and role diffusion with the concept of identity.

In the complex society of today, the individual must play

studies, based on responsible research, to contemporary American sociology. There is an excellent summary of the state of American sociology and the various contributions of the subdisciplines in the sociological field in *Sociology Today*, edited by Robert K. Merton and others (New York: Basic Books, 1959).

numerous roles: personal, vocational, intellectual. Furthermore, he is called upon to choose his roles, since he cannot fall back upon traditionally assigned roles that can be expected to remain stable. This is especially true in a mobile society where many children must be moved, as their fathers' jobs compel; this is true for both the manager's child and the child of the migrating farm worker, and as their fathers' economic rise or fall may dictate. Physical mobility may contribute something to the uniformity that distresses foreign observers of the American scene, but that uniformity also tends to make relationships shallow; identification may seem easy to establish in a standardized world, but such identification may well lack sustaining depth. A person who has built identity in this fashion may often find it impossible either to choose his roles or to reconcile them in all their complex variety.[7] Failure to achieve this reconciliation is frequent and leads to confusion in which role-playing itself may become impossible.

Often, the individual finds himself unable to set up long-range goals for himself. The many choices confronting him and his lack of adequate preparation to meet them and make decisions make it difficult, often impossible, for the individual to set long-range goals even in such personal matters as work, marriage, and the organization of his family life. His inability to identify himself properly with his roles, and the confusion and conflict between them, will ultimately lead to an inability to identify himself with his personal situation and the society around him. Truly, such a person does not know who he is, what he wants, where he belongs, where he would like to belong.

Because of the failure to achieve adequate individual identity, the boundary between the personal and the social tends to break down. In the old-fashioned inner-directed society, the individual who has incorporated parental and social commands could rely upon a strong superego to keep the disturbing id in check. He could identify with his community if only because he could rarely escape from it. Thus fixed, the community itself could develop a more differentiated form, often in esthetically satisfying architectural form. One need only live in European cities for a time to sense how important the image of the given surroundings is for the proper functioning of the individual in that society. The way a city has grown, as shown in its planning and architecture, is the outward and visible sign of the relationship between the individual and his society. Lack of balance in that relation is as

7 Ernst van den Haag and Ralph Ross, *Fabric of Society* (New York: Harcourt, Brace & Co., 1957), pp. 138-166.

evident in esthetic disharmony as in delinquency and un-happiness. To quote Ernst van den Haag,

> . . . without esthetic gratification man's capacity to give meaning to his life atrophies . . . the feeling of valuelessness, of futility—which oozes from our suburbs as much as it does from the city itself—is at the root of the *tedium vitae*, the listless and the restless boredom, the quiet or unquiet desperation which generates so many of our amusements, crimes and neuroses.[8]

The individual in transitional or other-directed societies lacks superego support for his identity. Consequently, he tends to seek identity through identification with a shifting group of his peers, whether these be classmates, fellow workers, or neighbors. Such shifting groups can provide only pseudo-identification, however; and the independence that characterizes an achieved individual identity can be attained only with the utmost difficulty. Rather than face himself, the individual submits to that lack of privacy which, again, seems so striking a characteristic of American life. Unfenced yards, picture windows, open-plan houses characterize a kind of life where the bathroom affords the only privacy generally respected (or indeed generally desired). In their search for identification, Americans involve themselves in so many organizations and groups, other than the frequently all-embracing corporation in which they work, that they often seem overwhelmed by the sheer weight of demand on their time.

Nevertheless, it cannot be said that the sense of belonging is on the increase in our society, as many observers say they believe; on the contrary it has declined and continues to do so. Modern man is losing any genuine sense of belonging because he finds it difficult to identify himself with the multitude of social roles he has to play. Current popular emphasis on belonging and "togetherness" signifies a longing rather than an achievement; something desired, not something possessed. When Housman wrote:

> I a stranger and afraid
> In a world I never made.

he was prophet, as poets are apt to be. Feeling alone in an alien world is now the emotional property of Everyman. So

---

[8] See Ernst van den Haag, "A Dissent from the Consensual Society" in *Daedalus*, Spring, 1960, p. 315. This article appears also in a slightly revised version in *Varieties of Modern Social Theory*, ed. Hendrik M. Ruitenbeek (New York: E. P. Dutton & Co., Inc., 1963).

many individuals feel not only isolated, cut off from friendship and acquaintance, to say nothing of love, but alone even in their intimacies that sociologists and psychotherapists are recognizing what the novelists have been describing for more than half a century, that loneliness[9] is a major distress of our time and one peculiarly related to that part of the identity problem which may be called the division between the individual and his world.

Persons who have experienced such division between their world and themselves find it increasingly difficult to choose a goal and decide what path they will take to reach it. The world has become too distant and frightening to allow him to identify himself with it. He may show a glib surface familiarity with his society and the cultural environment it provides, but he is still alienated from it. In recent decades the individual has come to feel that even participation in voluntary organizations, churches, study groups, and the like does not make him a part of his world. This experience leads him to consider the world as alien. Reflecting the insecurity of his time, he longs for security and a sense of belonging but finds neither obtainable in his present social environment and the situation which this presents to him as a person existing in the world.

Society provides contemporary Americans with a reasonable measure of economic security and material affluence.[10] Except for the aged, numbers of nonwhites, and the inhabitants of pockets of industrial decay and chronic unemployment, the struggle for bare existence is a thing of the past. To be in want, in the sense that the really poor are in want, is no longer too common an experience. Most persons no longer need cope with the material problems that beset them only twenty or thirty years ago. Instead the individual faces the hard inner reality of alienation, insecurity, and anxiety, all related to the diminution or even the loss of identity. Alienation occurs because of inability to achieve identification in a world where instability is at least the statistical norm. Old values have been eroded, new values develop too slowly to replace the loss effectively. Existential anxiety results and this affects both the individual and his society.

Some existential anxiety involves *rational* fear of danger and insecurity. Fear of this sort may lead to useful activity, as when a person becomes aware that his job is threatened

9 For an interesting study of the problems, see Margaret Mary Wood, *Paths of Loneliness* (New York: Columbia University Press, 1953; paperback edition, 1960).
10 See, for example, John Kenneth Galbraith's *The Affluent Society* (Boston: Houghton Mifflin Co., 1958).

with obsolescence by automation and therefore seeks training for another kind of work. A similar existential anxiety may affect large groups of people who feel threatened because of danger to their entire accustomed way of life: landed aristocracy confronted by plans for agrarian reform, for example, a farming population facing competition from foreign producers who can undersell them to the point of driving them out of their domestic markets, even a dominant regional group whose position is endangered by the upsurge of a lower caste—all these may show a characteristic existential anxiety. This kind of anxiety, with its roots in experiences common to many persons, must be distinguished from the neurotic anxiety rooted in irrational fears and guilts growing out of an individual's personal past.[11]

But there is another kind of existential anxiety, one common to all men, although all men are not equally aware of it. This kind of anxiety arises out of the condition of man's existence in the world. Philosophers, theologians, and poets have described their own confrontation of this anxiety and have given it many names. Basically, this aspect of existential anxiety can be understood in terms of the emotions a man experiences on walking in darkness, knowing, with a pang of immediacy, that the darkness was before one lived, that the darkness will be when one lives no longer, and that between these two darks of nonbeing men must lead their lives; they must dare and act although neither action nor daring may appear to be warranted.

Individual neurotic anxiety is not entirely divorced from existential anxiety, of course. The neurotic patient, too, lives in the world and is affected by all that affects and occurs in the world. But the individual's anxiety reflects the special, personal experience—notably his rearing in the family—which lies at the root of his neurosis. Such individual neurotic anxiety is connected with the problem of identity in ways which psychology, psychiatry, and psychoanalysis can handle, although, as we shall see, the ramifications of the identity problem have given a new dimension to psychotherapy. As Riesman observes, contemporary psychotherapists rarely see the classic hysteric patient, who expresses his psychological problems in physical symptoms. Rather, the therapist's patient suffers from aimlessness. He is often quite unable to describe

11 I should like to mention three of the psychological and philosophical studies of anxiety. The first is the classic study of Sigmund Freud, *The Problem of Anxiety* (New York: W. W. Norton & Co., Inc., 1936). Rollo May has written a fine study of the subject in *The Meaning of Anxiety* (New York: The Ronald Press Co., 1950). One of the best studies to date is Paul Tillich's *The Courage to Be* (New Haven: Yale University Press, 1952).

his problems, or to define them. He seems to know only that he is dissatisfied with his work, but can think of no other work that would be more satisfying; that his personal relations feel empty, but he has no idea how to fill them; that his life is without meaning, but all the traditional ways of making life meaningful seem irrelevant.

Such a patient needs a new vision, Riesman suggests.[12] In the terms of this book, this kind of patient needs not a new identity, but rather an identity *per se*. Even with the help of the psychoanalyst, the patient cannot really achieve this goal until contemporary technological society develops in such a way as to support the individual's effort to achieve *identification* and acquire a solid base from which he can develop an identity of his own.

Thus the problem of individual neurotic anxiety, insofar as it is associated with a person's failure to achieve identity, must be seen against the background of existential anxiety.

The study of existential anxiety goes beyond the scope of psychotherapy, for the therapist, by and large, concerns himself with the idiosyncratic personality structure of his patient. Existential anxiety, as has been said, is related to the structure of the society. It is through the channels offered by his society that the individual is most readily able to express and to cope with the anxiety he experiences because he exists. The channels that society provides include the whole system of relationships between the self and its special social environment as well as between the self and the culture as a whole. If these relationships are experienced as present and as relatively satisfactory, the person has achieved a measure of identity. If these relationships are not actually so experienced —even if the individual does not quite know what may be lacking in him—then existential anxiety begins to affect him. As that anxiety increases, the person's behavior shows a diminishing sense of identity and sometimes even shows a sense of its loss.

The situation just outlined presents a field for research by sociologists rather than by psychoanalysts[13] even though the analysts' clinical experience may give them a keen awareness of need for this particular kind of research. An increasing number of analysts are beginning to see patients whose prob-

---

12 See David Riesman's article "The Search for Challenge" in *New University Thought*, Spring, 1960. Vol. 1, no. 1, pp. 3-4.

13 To avoid misunderstanding, I should like to stress that it is extremely important, in my view, for the psychoanalyst to realize the effects of both individual and societal anxiety on his patient. He should, in short, acquaint himself with the patient's cultural setting. But this does not imply that both individual and societal anxiety are primarily problems for the analyst.

lems cannot be fully resolved in the context of the psycho-therapeutic interview.

In a period such as ours, marked by material comfort but existential disquiet, the individual is faced with a new set of problems that he can scarcely comprehend and that place him in a tragically dichotomous situation. He has lost the sense of identity experienced in the past. In its place comes worry, anxiety, and insecurity. Anxiety and insecurity are now a part of his existential self, for today the very notion of the self has changed. Its task is no longer to solve the meaning of past experience or even to seek new ideals to guide the future. *Utopian* has become a dirty word, along with *ideology* and *idealism*. Interest in political reform as a means of improving the human condition has dwindled although, in some respects and on some issues, there has been some revival of political activity by young people, especially in the colleges.[14]

With flagging concern with reform and the possibility of controlling or directing social change, man in contemporary society often sees himself as a being who can only submit to his experience and suffer. For relief of suffering, he reaches out for a pseudo-identity in a pseudo-reality. The desire to be accepted, the desire to belong and to belong to the right organization or group, often gives grotesque expression to man's effort to find a place for himself in our swiftly changing society.

Modern life is so highly organized that the individual has no opportunity to establish the pattern of his own identity because the organization imposes its pattern on him. In order to follow this pattern, he depends heavily on cues from his peers. All too often he has no strong identity, no inner security to fall back on. Small wonder that he seems to be in a continuous and almost desperate search for support and counsel. He seeks to identify himself with the many organizational patterns of his environment and society. Eagerly, he proclaims, to the world and himself, that involvement with these institutions is essential for the balanced, well-adjusted man, yet this involvement does not satisfy him. He seeks counsel from the clergyman and even the local banker; except in fairly large communities, he finds professional psychotherapy difficult to get (and often does not use it where it is available). He reads "inspirational" books, as he long has done, of course, but now those books are apt to inspire him in terms of a kind of do-it-yourself psychotherapy. Newspapers and magazines offer columns of consolation and counsel. These, too, are no

---

14 See on this point, Daniel Bell, *The End of Ideology* (New York: The Free Press of Glencoe, 1960) and David Riesman, "Where is the College Generation Headed?" *The Atlantic Monthly*, April, 1961.

new phenomena, but the old-time Advice to the Lovelorn column now uses a pseudo-psychological vocabulary. Counseling of this sort is found in English and Continental periodicals, incidentally, and there, too, it contributes to the public's confusion about psychoanalysis and psychology.[15]

So we can see the identity problem affecting all areas of modern experience, depleting the individual while it disturbs society. As both neurotic and existential anxiety are present in contemporary society, so that society is affected by both individual and societal anomie. Sociology owes the concept of anomie to the French sociologist, Emile Durkheim, who used the term to describe the phenomenon of social disorganization in an industrial society. Durkheim elaborated the concept of anomie in *Suicide* and *The Division of Labor in Society*. His ideas have particularly influenced the American sociologist Robert Merton. Among contemporary sociologists anomie is used to label the various forms of social disorganization in our society: Merton and his followers believe that crime and delinquency can be explained in terms of anomie. In this book, I use the term *societal anomie* rather than *anomie*, in order to make a clear distinction between personal anomie, (that is, the disorganization of personality), and societal anomie, or social disorganization taking place in society as a whole. Personal anomie is closely related to that aspect of the identity problem associated with neurotic anxiety. The concept of societal anomie is a useful tool in dealing with the prevalence of existential anxiety in our society. Once again, in discussing anxiety, insecurity, and anomie, we turn and turn again to the central concept of identity. Societal anomie cannot be discussed without relating its problems to what has been called the social identity, the characteristic style of a given society. Hence, we conjecture that identity crises occurring in our society are closely related to crises in organizations, institutions, and groups within it. In a later chapter we shall discuss more in detail the various aspects of anomie in our contemporary mass society. For the moment, it is sufficient to say that the increasing rate of delinquency and even of sexual deviant behavior may be considered as symptoms showing the prevalence of societal anomie.

Here again we see the dialectical character of identity. However we view the concept of identity or the problems in which it is involved, it is affected by interplay and playback.

[15] See *Harper's Magazine*, April, 1962, in which Maya Pines has an article on "Training Housewives as Psychotherapists," that opens new dimensions for accessible and inexpensive psychotherapy. See also "Dear Abby" in the *New York Journal-American* and "Evelyn Home" in *Woman* (London) as cases in point.

Contemporary men (unless they are either specially favored by circumstances or blunted by insensitivity) are affected by the depletion of or the search for identity. Loss and seeking both place the individual in continuous critical dialogue with himself and with society. For most men seek to communicate, and men uncertain of their identity find positive kinds of communication difficult to achieve. Men can share their disgusts; Edward Albee's *The American Dream* may be cited as an excellent example of the kind of exposure of middle-class American life (and most American life is middle class in fact or aspiration) that the middle-class American will pay to see.

Communicating hope is a matter different from sharing distaste. Indeed, as we have said, admitting to having any social hope or goal exposes a man to the charge of *idealism,* and in some intellectual circles, at least, a charge of burglary would be less derogatory. The failure of social goals to win allegiance and the frequently neurotic character of what allegiance they do win may be expressed in the numerous frictions and failures in the relationship between the individual and his society. Men who cannot cope with the complex societal and organizational pressures around them find no satisfaction in external idealistic goals, and often cannot relate to the world around them. Most of the remedies men seek in this situation tend to be inadequate. Neither psychoanalysis, to which the more sophisticated resort, nor the religious and pseudo-religious movements, nor the ultraconservative and the ultraradical political organizations, nor submissions to middle-class routine, nor for that matter a beatnik retreat to Greenwich Village, can create identity where none exists. The person who takes any of these paths may think he has learned how to bring meaning into his life, but he will soon find that this sense of purpose does not develop into a sense of identity.

Still another time, it becomes evident that the problem of identity is dialectical. The individual must engage in a continuous critical discussion with himself. He will, of course, get the material for his discourse from the outside, but it is he who must absorb the material. Ultimately, moreover, he finds himself alone and frequently unable to convey his inner feelings to others. Especially in the American other-directed society, and perhaps increasingly in European society, people are unable to project their own identity and assert themselves as individuals. One often wonders whether the inner-directed society (especially during the nineteenth century) was not a better setting for the individual who wished to communicate with *others.* Was that not the period when the function of the psychotherapist and the counselor was fulfilled by the good friend? The therapeutic value of being able, and willing, to communicate one's inner feelings to others has lessened in modern technological society. Consequently the individual finds himself through talking to himself rather than to the peers who, to so large a measure, supply his standards and sanctions.

Perhaps the very importance that psychotherapy has achieved in American life derives from the need for communication. Increasingly, however, the therapist's function has become reconciling the patient to his life rather than healing him of his neurotic suffering. Especially noteworthy is the contrast between his task and that of the analyst in Freud's time, when the analyst was scarcely concerned about the cultural and social setting of his age. The patient who presents himself with an identity problem testifies to the change that has taken place in our society. The therapist therefore must take account of the altered social context. Patients with identity problems must be made aware of the cultural background and content of their lives. The analyst must become acquainted with the patient's inner dialogue in order to discover the anxieties the patient experiences because he cannot play the roles that society requires him to assume.

Identity is established in the individual's day-to-day experience; there the significant breakdowns occur and there the patient needs help. But identity also involves the larger framework in which the patient's experiences occur. Thus, he needs more than the therapist's guidance. Through intensive questioning and subsequent reconciliation, the therapist can help the patient accept the need to live in this world. The sociologist's intensive observation and analysis of the social and cultural scene can deepen the therapist's approach to the patient and perhaps help at least the educated and intelligent patient approach himself. Thus the dialectical interchange may broaden to include not only patient, therapist, and social scientist but also artist and even political leader. If the contemporary individual, in therapy or out, is to surmount his identity crisis and find a way out of the desert of being without true identity, he needs inspiration, guidance, and even, perhaps, command of machinery for bringing social pressure.

We have seen that identity as a problem in our society has a number of aspects, but the crux of the matter is the actual weakening of, and search for, identity itself. The questions of insecurity, anxiety, and anomie that have been discussed are relevant, but do not provide a key to the essential meaning of the problem, for the significance of the concept of identity is quite separate from these issues. There have been times when individual anxiety was experienced without reference to the societal context. Of course people felt anxiety in medieval times and during the French and Industrial revolutions. But anxiety had not then crystallized as a social problem. In our contemporary mass culture, however, anxiety, insecurity, alienation, and anomie have become typical, and all are closely intertwined with the roots of this society's identity problem. Furthermore, identity and the other distresses we cite are experienced as problems only in a sophisticated "self-conscious" society.

The foregoing discussion of identity as a contemporary problem includes no detailed analysis, since it is intended to serve as a general introduction to the ramifications of the identity crisis in the structure of the self and society today. Later chapters will deal with specific aspects of the identity problem, one by one.

II. IDENTITY IN HISTORY

Since identity springs from the psyche's dealing with two factors in experience, identification and diversification, one may expect manifestations of identity to vary as changes in society affect the balance between those factors. Even to sketch the variations in identity that have occurred during the long human past requires far more space than a single chapter can compass. Accordingly, this discussion is limited to Western Europe during the centuries that have had the most immediate impact upon our own civilization. Greek, Roman, and Hebrew antiquity are omitted, not because those periods have been without influence—after all we owe even the way we find it "natural" to think to the work of Aristotle—but because exploration of identity during those thousands of years would carry us far afield and perhaps well beyond our solid information.

This chapter begins with the Middle Ages, therefore, and skims over highlights in the shifts of identity from the medieval period, through Renaissance and Reformation to the Industrial Revolution and the nineteenth century. So brief a survey must be cast in overly general terms, pleasing neither the historian nor the sociologist. Nevertheless, such a survey can help us understand how men's sense of identity varies between emphasis on identification through the living out of social roles and stress upon individuation through the growth of awareness that one is different from, and more than, those roles.

"The Middle Ages" is a term of rather vague reference; historians differ on the span of time it should label, and they have long ceased to think of the period as a simple and single entity about which one can make easy generalizations. The Middle Ages have been dismissed as a "thousand years without a bath"; they have been revered as the time when Europe was animated by a single creative faith. Here we are more modest, and less judgmental; we say only that between the ninth and the fourteenth centuries European societies do show a sufficient number of common characteristics to warrant our talking about a distinctively medieval identity.

Medieval men lived in a world of limited horizons, physical and intellectual. Their physical horizons were bounded by an agrarian way of life in which custom having the force of law tied the peasant to his birthplace and the craftsman to his trade. The higher classes had greater freedom of movement, but their intellectual horizons were only a little broader than those of their inferiors. Indeed, an intellectual climate dominated by the basic Christian myth of Fall and Redemption made self-imposed limitation a virtue. After all, man lost his place in Eden because Adam balked at the limits that God had imposed.

Medieval society seems designed to spare Adam's descendants the temptation to repeat the error. War and the Church offered channels of social mobility, to be sure. The peasant's restless sturdy son might go off to battle with his lord and gain something better than wounds or death for his service. The peasant's daughter might become a nun and even rise to importance in her order. The craftsman's son, or the peasant's, might learn rudimentary Latin in the Church's service, win the right to beg his way through a university, and get education enough to become priest or lawyer and so rise in the social scale.

Such mobility was unusual, however. Most medieval people found their identity in awareness of the social role prescribed by the estate into which they had been born. Men identified themselves as peasants, craftsmen, nobles, or clergy, not as separate unique individuals who happened to cultivate the land, weave cloth, fight, or perform church rituals. Their roles were made visible by dwelling and costume: the farmer's home clung close to the earth; the lord's castle crowned a hill when it could; the spire of the church rose toward the sky. Medieval towns stood behind walls that were symbol as well as protection: even merchants were expected to operate within fixed bounds, to charge no more than the "just price" for their goods, to share supplies with fellow merchants, to refrain from usury, that is, lending money at interest.

The clearly defined medieval social structure presented itself concretely in color and sound. Against the brown-gray of the peasants and the burghers' seemly black, nobles ruffled it in peacock blue and green and red. Bells clanged the time of day and the time of life, sounding to divide the church-man's hours, ringing joy for marriage, tolling to inform those who still lived that they too must die.

The structure thus delineated was firmly set in the ideologi-cal foundation provided by the Church. Continued participa-tion in its rites, continuous playing of the social roles it sanctioned, helped men establish a sense of identity in the very conviction that no roles were possible but those they had in-herited.[1]

That conviction was bolstered by the character of the medi-eval economy which had only minimal room for innovation. To be sure, technical improvements had occurred. The wind-mill was introduced from the Arab East. Stirrups and saddles made horses easier to ride; the horse collar made them useful for plowing. But changes came slowly. No man felt pressure to change, to rise in the world. All the pressures men did feel were in the other direction. The good man was he who knew his place and filled it, for all places were necessary, part of God's great scheme. Thus ran the sermons and homilies preached—when there was preaching—in parish churches. Thus ran the teaching and disputations in the universities. Reason and faith were God's equal gift and the revelation to faith could never in any way conflict with discoveries of reason. So Aquinas finally synthesized and expounded all the knowledge man had of the moral and intellectual world, and no other world mattered.

In such a social and intellectual context, choice was limited; thought restricted itself; and identity was identification rather than differentiation. As Erich Fromm puts it: "The social order was conceived of as a natural order, and being a definite part of it gave man a feeling of security and belonging."[2]

Our image of medieval man's security owes a good deal to nineteenth-century protests against the disruptive impact of the French and the Industrial revolutions. The German and French romanticists, who found in the Enlightenment the roots of the upheavals following 1789, harked back to the Middle Ages as the "good time gone." In *Past and Present,* one sees Carlyle using the Middle Ages as a club with which to beat his contemporaries. Fromm himself sometimes seems to be playing a similar game.

[1] Johan Huizinga, *The Waning of the Middle Ages* (New York: Doubleday Anchor Books, 1956), pp. 9-10.
[2] *Escape from Freedom* (New York: Rinehart, 1941), pp. 41-42.

Nevertheless, it does appear that medieval society did give men greater support in establishing and maintaining identity than subsequent Western societies have done. If a medieval man or group of men could not find themselves through identification with the world as presented to them, however, they had to reject the whole set of inherited values. A medieval man felt no liberty to choose among the values by which the society lived. He had to earn his living within the system of manor, guild, and gown. He had to live within the Christian moral scheme and the administration of Christianity by the Church. He had to think in Aristotelian intellectual conventions as those were interpreted by the universities. He had to take the given *as* it was given. Or he had to reject it all.

And since total rejections did occur, it is fair to see them as evidence that medieval men did experience identity crises. Such crises may be inferred behind the growth of heresies as well as in such medieval phenomena as the Crusades and the flagellation mania. Heresy illustrates conflict between the two aspects of identity: the need for identification and the need for individuation. Tension between the two produces the characteristically medieval identity crises. The restive medieval man suffered because his social framework left insufficient opportunity for individuation; in contrast, the restive modern man suffers because his society demands individuation, imposes identification, and gives him inadequate support for developing either.

Medieval people who found themselves at odds with the assumption that their roles in the social order were part of the eternal scheme of things tended to seek another order rather than try to find a new place in the existing framework. Thus, as Norman Cohn points out in *The Pursuit of the Millennium*,[3] the poor were particularly receptive to preachers who warned that the final days were at hand, the days of judgment when the first should be last and the last first; that is, when the present social order should be reversed and a new order come to replace it.

Similarly, during the twelfth and thirteenth centuries, many showed their discontent with life in the enclosure of their assigned social roles by seeking spiritual growth in ways other than those the Church prescribed. They felt their social roles to be more constricting than fulfilling, but they did not express

---

3 Norman Cohn in his book, *The Pursuit of the Millennium* (New York: Harper Torchbooks, 1961), gives an excellent survey of the various revolutionary, messianic movements in medieval Europe. See also his article, "The Cult of the Free Spirit: A Medieval Heresy Reconstructed," in *Psychoanalysis and the Psychoanalytic Review*, Spring, 1961, Vol. 48, no. 1, p. 51.

their discontent as individual persons in the name of their individuality. Rather, they rejected one identification—as members of the Catholic Church—in order to replace it with another, as members of a heretic group. Yet that attempt to choose identification was an assertion of one's uniqueness even in the face of death.

For abandoning the medieval religious solution was heresy; and heresy was an offense against God and a threat to the community. God had appointed the Church to tell men what to believe and how to show their faith. Refusal to behave as the Church required was disobedience to God. Since men were weak and likely to be seduced by heretics, communities tolerating heresy imperiled the souls of their members and undermined the sanctions of the social order besides. When the Church discovered heretics and found them persistent in refusing to return to obedience, it gave them over to the secular arm for disposal.

The ideas of the chief heresies of the Middle Ages indicate something of the strain of maintaining identification with inherited social roles. Heresy was especially prevalent in the more economically developed areas of Europe: northern Italy, southern France, Flanders, the Rhine Valley. The heretics generally denounced the wealth and luxury of the clergy and attacked their monopoly of dispensing the Sacraments, the means of grace, and of religious knowledge. In short, they preached a return to earlier Christian practice.

An observer of crassly economic orientation might underscore the relationship between merchants' desire to accumulate capital and their desire to have a less costly path to salvation. On the other hand, one might remark that the people closest to the money economy, which was already operating to undermine the medieval social structure, were those who experienced greatest need of a new religious outlook, a new means of relating to themselves and to others: a new identity.

Sometimes medieval dissenters, such as the Cathars, went beyond the attempt to revert to primitive Christianity. The Cathars turned to a Manichaean dualism, which urged men to free the spirit from its fleshly bondage to evil by following the road to perfection, that is, to own no property, to take no oaths, to tell no lies, to eat no animal food, and to abstain from sex. The earnest Cathar who was unable to follow that path entirely lived sparely, fasted often, sang hymns, prayed, and listened to sermons.

This grim creed won a sufficient number of converts in the cultivated and wealthy region ruled by the Counts of Toulouse to make it necessary to preach a crusade against the Albigensians, as the local Cathars were called. After nearly half a century of struggle, the Cathars were finally beaten by the sword; rooted out by the Inquisition—which found peculiarly sober lives cause for suspicion—and won over by Catholic preaching.[4]

The psychoanalyst may well wonder whether the power of such life-renouncing doctrine as the Cathars' does not offer testimony to the relative weakness of the ego in medieval man and to the necessity, therefore, of a peculiarly harsh superego to keep powerful id forces in control.

Again, the inflexible character of the medieval social order itself may reflect the strength of id elements and account for the bizarre character of deviant behavior. Thus, members of the lay Order of the Flagellants flogged themselves and each other in public until spectators caught the contagion, whipped themselves till they bled, and burst into riot, first robbing Jews and then other citizens until the authorities finally intervened. Such phenomena indicate that medieval identity was maintained through the dominance of the superego in the character structure; when the achieved identity could no longer endure superego restraints, id forces burst out with special violence. Since one cannot examine the psychic structure of people who are centuries dead and whose behavior has not been scientifically recorded, such comment can be no more than speculation. Yet scanning what records we do have seems to permit some tentative conclusions.

During the Middle Ages, the dominant ideology restricted intellectual approaches to reality. The ego was not socially encouraged to develop. Inquiry into the natural world, for example, was sometimes equated with the practice of black magic. The partisans of Aristotle's natural philosophy did overcome early attempts to forbid its study, but his statements about the natural world were transmuted into truths which were not to be baldly confronted by actuality. Such an attitude in the society could not but tend to lessen the effectiveness of ego activity when id forces asserted themselves against the dictates of the superego.

And superego demands often ran counter to reality. Consider, for example, the problem of clerical celibacy. Buddhism as well as Christianity requires its monks and nuns to refrain from sexual activity, but only the Roman Church required all members of its clergy to lead celibate lives, a restriction that the Orthodox Church imposed only upon the upper levels of its hierarchy. One might expect the demand for chastity to be more than many a priest could meet, especially if his

4 Fernand Niel, *Albigenses et Cathares* (Paris: Presses Universitaires, 1959), pp. 54-55.

vocation were acquiescence in family expectation rather than truly free choice.

Thus, it is not surprising that Peter Damiani's denunciations of the clergy make historians eager to leave them in the "decent obscurity of a learned tongue." Eude Rigaud, Archbishop of Rouen, offers interesting testimony in his surveys of the state of the Church in his diocese between 1248 and 1269. At Cotignes, the priest was reproved for gambling as well as unchastity; at another town, the local priest took women of evil lives with him when he went to fairs and haunted taverns. A third priest was actually unfrocked because he had not only fathered numerous bastards, but lent money at usury, and made wax figures for use in witchcraft. In the priory at Ovilla, the prior was drunken and given to women. The nuns were careless of their prayers at the convent at Villa Arcelli, they perfumed their veils and misbehaved with both clergy and laymen.[5] Solemn official inquiry—Rigaud's is only one among many accounts—thus bears out the picture conveyed by the seamy yarns of the *fabliaux* and the less seemly narratives in the *Canterbury Tales*.

Imposition of celibacy may have had motives other than fear and hatred of sexuality. A celibate clergy could not convert Church property into personal and hereditary feudal domains, for example. Yet hostility to sex has been peculiarly strong in the scheme of Christian morality and unconscious response to that antagonism shows itself in such medieval phenomena as the witchcraft persecutions and the proceedings against the Knights Templar.

The wealth of the great crusading order might tempt a more scrupulous monarch than Philip the Fair, but the acts attributed to the Templars by the prosecutors who finally procured the dissolution of the Order in 1314 show what the law-abiding hankered to do rather more accurately than they report what the accused had done. For the procedure here, like that in the witchcraft trials, entailed putting questions to the suspects and torturing them until they gave affirmative answers. So the Templars were charged with renouncing women only that they might corrupt youths, with abandoning Christianity for idolatry, with insulting the Cross, and with treating the Host as a live person to be shamed and degraded.

The witchcraft persecutions offer more vivid testimony to the irruption of id elements. During the early Middle Ages, clerical authorities advised that those who accused people as witches be treated as malicious gossips and that those accusing

[5] H. O. Taylor, *Medieval Mind* (London: The Macmillan Co., 1938), Vol. I, pp. 490-496.

themselves in confession be dealt with as what we call hysterics. Gradually, this opinion receded. By the fourteenth century, after the bubonic plague had devastated Europe, the Church authorities contended that witches had power as well as bad intentions. The churchmen who were charged with the duty of extirpating witchcraft accused the suspect of renouncing their faith and showing that renunciation by serving the devil as sexual partners in deviantly fantastic ways. The widespread use of such manuals as the *Malleus Maleficarum,* which told inquisitors what questions to ask, makes one wonder whether the testimony in witch trials bears witness to the behavior of the defendants or the sexual fantasies of the prosecutors. Some scholars, however, are persuaded that the pattern that can be drawn from testimony in witch trials all over Europe shows that witchcraft actually was an independent religion, survivor of ancient fertility cults.[6] If this be true, the apparent upsurge of the cult during the last centuries of the Middle Ages and the transition to modern times (the high-water mark of witchcraft persecutions came in the fifteenth century and continued into the sixteenth) may point to the development of a real identity crisis within the weakening framework of medieval life.

Although that framework had been supportive of identity, as has been shown earlier, and though it maintained people in serene awareness of who they were, within that framework, people knew themselves as members of estates rather than in full individual separateness. To be sure, the individual was important, for every man embodied a soul and each human soul was the concern of God, protagonist in what Santayana has called "the Christian epic" of fall, sin, salvation. Yet medieval emphasis lay on the soul as one of a class rather than as an individual. A man might take a unique path toward damnation, but he was most likely to be saved if he behaved in the appointed ways. Medieval men found themselves, as it were, by placing themselves within traditional patterns of relationship with others. Efforts to choose other than traditional patterns of relations with men and God were punished, for no man could be permitted to damn himself and pervert his neighbors.

As new influences began to affect the medieval economy and particularly as men made increasing use of money, the character of medieval life altered. Europe, and particularly Catholic Christian Europe, regained access to the Mediterranean and its more highly developed areas, Byzantium and the

6 Margaret Murray, *God of the Witches* (London: Faber & Faber, 1952).

Moslem East. The subsequent growth of towns created a market, and the spread of a market economy undermined self-contained manorial agriculture as the basis of economic life. With a market available, the gentry came to prefer tenants who paid rent in money to serfs who paid dues in labor and in kind. The prosperous craftsman tried to win a greater share in the local market for himself. Merchant and banker extended their range of operations to the point where town and guild regulations were a halter on their enterprises. Slowly, between the thirteenth and fifteenth centuries, the stability of the medieval world was shaken.

Many factors besides the growth of a money economy helped break the medieval "cake of custom" and contributed to the widening of horizons that culminated, physically, in the finding of the Western Hemisphere and the discovery that men had found a new, an unknown world. In the Crusades, medieval Europe had encountered a foreign culture, its superior in many respects. Partly as a result of contact with the Moslem world, Europe gradually enlarged its acquaintance with its Greek heritage and made that acquaintance more intimate. Europeans had sharpened their wits in university and law courts and improved their techniques in workshop and on the land.

Change and growth in the medieval economy and intellectual climate were reflected in the historical movements we label "Renaissance" and "Reformation." As these movements changed and reflected change in the minds of men and the behavior of society, identity, too, changed. Men still tried to find themselves, to establish identities, but they searched in new ways, and they found new persons.

Medieval man seems to blend with his social background, to be one with his "state," his apportioned role in society. Even after taking account of historical studies that show how much of the medieval survived into the sixteenth century, one is aware of the difference: Renaissance man stands away from his background, a splendid figure in splendid round.

The Middle Ages had "individuals," of course; one need only name St. Bernard, Eleanor of Acquitaine, Peter Abelard, or Jeanne d'Arc to show that. But the Renaissance is distinctively the era of *l'uomo singolare,* as the Italian has it. Even more, the Renaissance is the era of the whole man, so dazzling in his completeness, that no one role could absorb him and society often seemed a mere backdrop to show him off. Who has not read Leonardo da Vinci's letter offering his services to Ludovico Sforza, Duke of Milan? And what is more amazing than knowing that Leonardo could make good every one of his claims? The evidence of Leonardo's *Notebooks* is even more impressive than a statement, which was necessarily a horn blown in his own praise, for they record that most intimate of communications, a creative man's conversation with himself. Here we see Leonardo, engineer, anatomist, mathematician, chemist, geologist, astronomer, inventor of the Rorschach, and defender of the honor of the art of painting.[7]

But it is not only the versatility and achievements of Leonardo and his contemporaries that so astonish; it is the fullness of their presence in existence, what the Italian Renaissance called *virtu,* the capacity for showing oneself a man. The scholar and the artist lived in the world and their world had use for all their powers. Machiavelli helped make history before he narrated it; he practiced politics before he wrote what some call a basic treatise on the getting and keeping of political power. Lorenzo de Medici is described as eminent in statesmanship, classical learning, the knowledge of agriculture, and the practice of poetry in the vulgar tongue. He won the title of Magnificent by spending much of his banker family's money in supporting the artists and scholars who made Florence a center of art and learning.[8]

Nor was this richness of life characteristic of the Italian Renaissance alone. Where the new learning and the new art came, the complete man came too. Rubens, for example, was diplomat as well as painter. In distant Hungary, constantly threatened by the Turks, Matthias Corvinus understood learning as well as war; he founded universities while he fought the enemy. And in Elizabeth Tudor's England, Sir Walter Raleigh was explorer, navigator, businessman, poet, and courtier.

Such citing of names and lives is no mere accumulation of anecdote. Rather, it illustrates the new shape that identity was assuming in the Western world. We have seen how an increasingly complicated and varied economy and a growing body of knowledge offered man an increasing range of choices. More important, perhaps, as a money economy spread and eroded older institutions, the medieval way of life became less supportive. During the late Middle Ages, the financial needs of popes and kings offered new opportunities to the owners of capital, and risks unheard of earlier. Indeed, the bankruptcy of King Edward III of England in 1346 ruined the Florentine banking houses of Bardi and Peruzzi and their fall may have opened the way for the rise of the Medici. Certainly, the experience of the fallen houses made the capitalists of Florence

7 Leonardo da Vinci, *Notebooks,* E. Macurdy, ed. (London: Duckworth & Co., 1906), pp. 158, 162, 173.

8 G. F. Young, *Medici* (New York: Modern Library, 1930), pp. 149-150.

understand the meaning of "put not your faith in princes"; henceforth, they tended to invest in the wool trade and other commercial ventures. Bankers in the Low Countries and the Germanies put capital into mining as well as trade and manufacture. By the fifteenth century, mining was a modern business, employing water-driven pumps, hoists, and even trip-hammers, as well as large amounts of capital. The glory of the Renaissance was paid for by profits as well as loot and taxes.

On the intellectual level, meanwhile, the late Middle Ages had laid the foundation for the New Learning. The universities may have been somewhat inhospitable to the novelties of humanism, but they had fostered intellectual interests and we may conjecture that they had also produced a number of educated youths who could find few suitable professional openings, and who were even more inclined than the wandering students of the earlier Middle Ages to become "scholars at large," as it were. This trend, too, the Renaissance encouraged.

Greek learning had not perished, moreover; the fall of Constantinople did not, as historians once thought, release a flood of classic literary beauty that civilized the barbarian West. Contact with the Moslem East had roused interest in Aristotle. Gradually, a new concern with the classics wakened. Contact with exiles from Byzantium and with scholars in the suites of diplomats further roused European concern with its Greek heritage. By the fifteenth century, scholars searched for Greek manuscripts, worked at translating them into Latin, developed techniques for the study and comparison of texts. Such study made critical treatment of the written word increasingly common if not increasingly respectable. The revival of antiquity may have strengthened the authority of the past in some respects, but it also widened the choice among authorities. Cardinal Bembo, for example, counseled a friend against reading St. Paul's Epistles, lest he corrupt his Latin style.[9]

Renaissance learning made men re-examine the documents upon which prevailing intellectual authority was said to rest. Scholars turned to Scripture in Greek and even in Hebrew; they read the early Church Fathers with new interest. The northern humanists, particularly, became intimate with primitive Christianity as well as with pagan poetry. And intimacy with Christian sources unsettled more minds than the love of Plato.

The development of Renaissance science also showed that traditional learning did not encompass all possible knowledge. There were more things in the world than Aristotle had

[9] John Addington Symonds, *Renaissance in Italy* (New York: Modern Library, 1935), Vol. I, p. 511.

known, and some of what he had known was not so. The introduction of gunpowder in the fourteenth century did more than change methods of making war; it impelled men to fresh study of physics and mathematics. Improved lenses—a medieval technical innovation, incidentally—widened men's ability to see both the great and small, the stars in the sky and the crawling life in seemingly limpid fluids. Nevertheless, the new scientific learning did not really affect the medieval picture of the universe until Copernicus formulated a new cosmography and Kepler provided some of the observations that made that world view clearer.

Learning and art and science, the high culture of the Renaissance, was limited to the few, to be sure. Some patrons of Renaissance learning and even many humanists looked down on printed books—knowledge was not to be profaned by easy reproduction—but they could not keep the fruit of their labor to themselves. For more and more people had learned to read, and printing brought books and ideas into the possession of increasing numbers. Renaissance art was embodied in buildings that all men could see and Renaissance paintings and statues adorned those buildings. Although more and more portraits and easel pictures were painted, the patrons of Renaissance artists still glorified themselves by making public buildings glorious.

Thus, as the Renaissance developed, an increasing number of men could no longer rest comfortably in the cradle of identification. They had to seek identity in other ways. People became aware of themselves in terms of a unique inner element that had to be brought into being and expressed rather than in terms of the complete soul with which they, like all other men, had been born. Thus, people began to identify themselves in terms of the special and particular as well as the social and general; they sought to establish an individuation as well as identification. In a supportive social framework, particularly, identification may occur by a sort of assimilation. Individuation, on the other hand, requires active choice even though, in certain social groups, pressure may force choice in a particular direction.

In one sense, then, individuation demands that a person create himself, whereas identification requires only that he find himself. In contrast to the Middle Ages, the Renaissance is not only a period of whole men but also a period of men who might be called self-made. Some, such as the Sforza or the Maletesta in Italy, are predatory in type; others carried the methods of the *condottieri* into the intellectual realm. The humanist lords of learning had something of the assertive individuality of the men who rose by the sword and their shrewdness in selling it. The humanists were feted (when they were not forced to beg); they frightened princes (when they did not seek refuge from charges of heresy behind some despot's ample robe); their arrogance was such that a sixteenth-century moralist could cite them as an instance of the sin of pride, *Superbia*.[10]

The Renaissance had more in common with the Middle Ages than was once generally recognized: on careful view, even the most abrupt turn in the stream of history appears as a curve rather than a jerk. Nevertheless, both in idea and in practice, the Renaissance man experiences his identity in a different fashion from his medieval predecessor. He was less bound to an inherited status; he felt more free to move socially. We may take as an indication of increased social mobility the popularity of Castiglione's *Courtier*, most notable among the books that described the difficult art of getting along at court, perhaps in a status to which one had not been born. Since Renaissance man was more mobile than medieval man and less identified with inherited or ascribed social roles,[11] he was under correspondingly greater pressure to find a place of his own. Such a person might be expected to be anxious, to experience some degree of alienation, and to seek comfort in familiar ways. Reverence for antiquity did not preclude response to Christian earnestness. In the storm of repentance that Savonarola's preaching roused in Florence, for example, women burned their rouge, gamblers their cards, and gallants their lovers' portraits. Artists went into monasteries, or, like Botticelli, gave up the Greek myths and Aphrodite in order to paint the Virgin with the Child whose death her mystically enlightened eyes foresee.

If politics were unscrupulous and religion unbridled during the Renaissance, men paid no less attention to love, which often seems to have been practiced as the most beguilingly dangerous of games, combat between possessor and seducer, husband and lover (more rarely between guardian-brothers and suitor, since unmarried girls were not visible in good society). The lady was presumed accessible, if not frail. Enjoying her meant victory; leaving the lover in peaceful occupation meant shame for the husband. Hence the tradition

[10] Jacob Burckhardt, *The Civilization of the Renaissance in Italy* (New York: Harper Torchbooks, 1958).
[11] Wallace K. Ferguson, *Renaissance in Historical Thought* (Boston: Houghton Mifflin Company, 1948), pp. 231-232, citing Alfred von Martin, *Sociology of the Renaissance* (New York: Harper Torchbooks, 1963).

of poison and the assassin's dagger as the earthly risks of honorably adulterous love.[12]

The platonic tradition of ideal love did not die, however; Bembo dedicated his dialogues on the subject to Lucrezia Borgia[13] and some popes made war to increase the possessions of those who were tactfully called their nephews. And although Sodoma was not the only Renaissance painter to portray youths of ambiguous beauty, he did have a unique ability to show Hylas the minion of Heracles in the shape of the tortured seductiveness of St. Sebastian.[14]

As the Renaissance laid fresh stress on individuality, the search for identity took on an altered psychic dimension. We have conjectured that, during the Middle Ages, identity was linked with strong superego elements and that id forces broke bonds in wild outbursts of fanaticism and violence. Similar forces were evident during the Renaissance, but rebellion against the restraints of the ecclesiastical system, particularly, tended to express itself not in heresy but in religious indifference or a rather dilettante syncretism. The members of the Platonic Academy at Florence, for example, tried to reconcile Christian doctrine with what they understood Plato to have taught. Where northern humanists were genuinely troubled by the corruption they saw in the Church, the great Italian scholar, Lorenzo Valla, is said to have silenced persistent inquisitors into his opinions with "I believe as mother church believes; to be sure, she knows nothing, but I believe as she believes."[15] And because Valla was under the protection of the King of Naples, he escaped unpunished either for his impudence or for the textual studies by which he proved that the document upon which the popes based their claim to temporal dominion in Italy was a forgery.

The inquiring spirit that made research such as Valla's possible indicates that the conditions of Renaissance learning gave new scope for the ego to deal with reality. Although the literary authority of antiquity was added to the authority of the medieval religious framework, the very presence of two authorities with different frames of reference presented an opportunity for choice and hence greater scope for ego activity. Economic and political changes, too, offered men new opportunities to achieve identity in terms of both individuation and identification. But these opportunities were accompanied by new pressures: instead of enjoying, as it were, the identity through identification that had come all but

12 Young, *op. cit.*, pp. 251-252.
13 Burckhardt, *op. cit.*, p. 73.
14 Symonds, *op. cit.*, p. 815.
15 *Ibid.*, p. 449.

naturally to most men in the Middle Ages, an increasing number of persons were now confronted with the possibility of choice. This very possibility might give rise to the kind of tension and anxiety that may be interpreted as an identity crisis. Hence, although Burckhardt calls the Renaissance paganizing, he also points out how responsive many people were to what we call religious revivalism and how they sought relief in superstition as well as in the practice of their inherited religion.[16]

In the experience of the Reformation, identity crises play a more important part still. Erik Erikson, indeed, sees the Reformation itself growing out of an identity crisis occurring in a man who mirrors his age.[17] Martin Luther's father, for example, was a peasant who had prospered by leaving the land for the advanced industry of mining. And we may well think that Luther succeeded where earlier rebels against the Church had failed because he presented his religious views to persons no longer in the context of the medieval social structure. The impact of the growth of a money economy during the late Middle Ages has already been sketched. But other significant fissures had appeared in the medieval framework. Within the Church, dissension had gone so far during the fourteenth century as to remove the papal court from Rome to Avignon for nearly three quarters of a century. At Avignon, the Church improved its administration and its financial position, but it tended to lose spiritual prestige as it gained worldly efficiency. From everywhere within Western Christendom came demands for reform and reunion. Union was restored: the papal court moved back to Rome and the papacy regained dominance in the Church, but the attempt at reform dwindled and faded after the prolonged and futile efforts of the Council of Constance.

Meanwhile, a new focus of allegiance had arisen in France, England, and even Spain. The new national monarchies were able to establish a considerable measure of control over Church appointments and fund raising in their territories. In the Germanies, on the other hand, where central authority had diminished rather than increased, the Church found it easier to raise money. Yet increasingly, its efforts were felt as exploitative. Thus, when Pope Julius II decided to pull down the ancient basilica of St. Peter in order to replace it with the great building now known by that name, he laid the foundation for the Protestant Revolt. To his successor, Pope Leo X, the German towns and principalities seemed a fertile source

16 Burckhardt, op. cit., pp. 479, 484.
17 Erik H. Erikson, Young Man Luther (New York: W. W. Norton & Company, Inc., 1962), p. 22.

of money for the project. Hence he offered special indulgences to those making payment as indication of intention to reform. Sale of the new indulgences was promoted in a thoroughly businesslike manner with the Archbishop of Mainz managing the project on shares, and his agent preached the indulgences in a tone not too different from that used to tell modern middle-aged women that unguents will restore their lost youth.

Luther's theses attacking the indulgences were merely the flame set to fuel already piled high: long-standing demands for reform and the work of such humanists as Erasmus, who provided new intellectual and ideological material upon which to base demands for a renovation of religion. Thus Luther was able to win from the princes the solid support upon which the practical success of the Protestant Revolt depended.[18]

As a result of the undermining of the medieval social structure, an increasing number of people experienced identity crises. In order to resolve such crises it was necessary to replace or reconstitute the framework, and in greater or less degree the Reformation achieved this objective. Superego forces, weakened during the slow breakdown of the medieval world, further shaken during the Renaissance transition, and severely disturbed by the Protestant Revolt, were finally restored in what Max Weber has called the Protestant Ethic. By evoking the Catholic Counter-Reformation, the Protestant Revolt finally forced the reform within the Church that previous centuries of effort had failed to accomplish. On the other hand, the Protestant Revolt resisted attempts to suppress it as earlier heresies had been suppressed. It succeeded in winning political support at least in part because more individuals were aware of an increasing need of new ways in which they could learn who they were and acquire a sense of belonging with others.

As the new mode of experiencing identity emerged in the sixteenth and seventeenth centuries, we see a new role for both ego and superego. The success of the Lutheran Revolt made it less and less possible to impose religious uniformity, to tell the innovator in northern Europe, "Thus far and no farther." To be sure, rulers did try to force all their subjects to accept the true faith, which was the ruler's. Catholics burned Protestants and Protestants burned each other as well. For religion could not be left merely to private choice.

Yet despite, or perhaps even because of, the perils, individuals exercised a greater range of intellectual choice. A

18 H. O. Taylor, *Thought and Expression in the Sixteenth Century* (New York: The Macmillan Company, 1920), p. 257.

man could now select his identification by choosing the faith with which he wanted to affiliate. And by that choice he tended to achieve greater individuation. In order to exercise freer choice in religion, moreover, political activity was often necessary. Although, after the suppression of the Peasants' Revolt, the Lutheran phase of the Reformation was politically passive, the Calvinist phase tended to be far more aggressive and creative on that level. Lutheranism made its greatest advances in the politically backward Germanies and Scandinavia. Calvinism was most effective in such areas as England, Geneva, Scotland, and the Netherlands, which were somewhat active politically as well as economically advanced. It is not without significance that England and the Netherlands, at least, were fortunately situated for drawing profit from the new areas that Portugal and Spain had opened for European trade. While commerce in the Germanies was being affected by changes in overseas trade routes as well as afflicted by war, commerce was expanding in the Netherlands and England. And to these areas the Calvinists offered an intellectual framework peculiarly suited to support identity in an increasingly money-oriented world.

During the Middle Ages, concern for making money had required apology. In contrast, as Max Weber points out in *The Protestant Ethic and the Spirit of Capitalism*,[19] the Calvinists developed the concept that earning money was "the result and expression of virtue and proficiency in calling," that is, the performance of religious duty.[20] In such a doctrine the great traders, and the industrialists who were to follow them, found an ideological framework within which they could experience their identity. The framework was religious, to be sure, for no more than the Renaissance did the Reformation cast off all medieval ways of relating to the world. If men thought about themselves and society at all, they still thought in terms of God's plan and man's duty to live in accordance with that plan. Nevertheless, because making money requires innovation, the European society that

---

[19] Max Weber, *The Protestant Ethic and the Spirit of Capitalism* (New York: Charles Scribner's Sons, 1958), pp. 53–54.

[20] Weber notes that Luther used the German word *Beruf* ("calling") in a sense it had never before possessed. Nor is there any precise equivalent for it either in antiquity or in Roman Catholic writing. It appears in Luther's translation of Ecclesiasticus 11:21, "Trust in the Lord and abide in thy *Beruf*." From this translation and from Luther's use of the word elsewhere it became a standard word in the vocabulary of the Protestant peoples. It is interesting to note the Greek word that Luther translates "calling" means "toil." From his use of the term elsewhere it is clear that he is here thinking of the work of the secular, everyday life as a God-appointed task, a calling.

developed as the Reformation matured was far less tradition-bound than those which preceded it. Men could no longer experience identity merely as a social "given," they now had to experience their relationship to themselves and others in more individual terms.

Increasingly, in Western Europe at least, men internalized the ideological changes that the Reformation entailed. These might be summed up as greater independence and a more acute sense of responsibility for one's life in this world and one's fate in the next. Instead of feeling bound to, and supported by, the dogmas of the Roman Church, for example, men rested their faith upon their own reading of the Scriptures. And "Seest thou a man diligent in his business? He shall stand before kings" seemed a more relevant text than "Consider the lilies of the field, they toil not, neither do they spin, yet Solomon in all his glory was not arrayed like one of these."

Thus, one might say that the cash nexus tended to replace the umbilical cord as the primary societal tie. Increasingly, after the Reformation, men identified themselves in terms of their relation to money. They internalized the commands and sanctions of the Protestant Ethic: work, for the night is coming, and lay up treasure on earth to show yourself worthy of admission to heaven.

The psychoanalyst who contrasts the epoch of the Reformation with the Middle Ages or even with the Renaissance is tempted to infer oral ways of relating yielding to anal patterns. Men grasped for identification; they no longer simply received it. The new Protestant churches had no place for the Madonna and her nursling. Their God may have given His son for man's redemption, but He shared power with neither saint in heaven nor head of church on earth. And increasingly, man stood alone before God as soon as he was to stand alone before his society. By the seventeenth century, many Western men were developing a new relationship to themselves.

That relationship and the modification of identity it represents became clearer during the next two hundred years until finally, sociologists might say that men knew themselves increasingly as individuals and decreasingly in terms of stable social roles. And, for many, knowing oneself as an individual meant feeling oneself in opposition to society. The *bourgeois* might identify himself in terms of his social role, a role requiring him to orient his life around money, for he had fought for and won the right to a leading place in society. But the artist and many an intellectual—successor to the humanist "scholar at large"—found his identity through opposition to a society that offered him no role he was willing to accept. Thus identification became more and more difficult for a growing number of individuals and identity was experienced primarily in terms of individuation.

But if individuation is to be fully achieved, it requires freedom to develop. And freedom is an eighteenth- and nineteenth-century watchword. Particularly it is a watchword of the two key phenomena of those centuries, the French and the Industrial revolutions.

The roots of these upheavals go back into the seventeenth century, when modern science came into being. It was in the eighteenth century, however, and in considerable degree as the result of the work of the French *philosophes* that the new science, and especially the Newtonian view of the universe, became the property of the average educated man. The eighteenth century, too, transformed into common European property the political theory that had been developed to justify the seventeenth-century revolutions by which England, having rid itself of the Stuarts, established its unwritten constitution, a severely limited monarchy in which the rights of the subject rested on procedural law.[21] And in 1763, James Watt and Matthew Boulton set up an iron foundry in which a trip-hammer was operated by steam power. Power was applied to manufacturing as well as to mining and the world of modern industrial technology had finally come to birth.

If we look at the French Revolution, we can agree with de Tocqueville that it had many aspects of a religious movement, particularly in respect to its propaganda for the gospel summed up in the classic phrase: *liberté, égalité, fraternité.* In spite of the failure of the First French Republic, the Revolution cut Western Europe's remaining ties to the medieval world. Whatever political retrogression might occur, absolutist monarchy would henceforth be an anachronism; and remnants of medieval systems of land holding would be seen as exploitation.

More relevant to the problem with which this book is concerned was the impact of the Revolution upon the way in which men perceived their identity. During the decades of warfare in which the Revolution and then Napoleon battled the forces of an older Europe, many men realized their identity in action. Others, notably Goethe, pursued in their lives the ideal of the complete man that characterizes the Renaissance. But when the dust had settled, as it were, when Napoleon was in exile at St. Helena and the Bourbons were restored in France, Spain, and Naples and the Emperors of Russia and

---

21 Alexis de Tocqueville, *The Old Regime and the French Revolution* (New York: Doubleday Anchor Books, 1955), p. 11.

Austria sat on more comfortable thrones, the young men of Europe, the poet-creators of sensibility, particularly, sought identity in terms of individuation and found individuation in freedom from the claims of society. Where Voltaire had said *écrasez l'infame*, the young Romantics cried *épater les bourgeois*. The middle class, not the Church, was the infamous object of their wrath, for it was the middle class that held power, and to its prescriptions most creative minds refused allegiance. Thus, perhaps for the first time in Western history, many intellectuals refused to give their allegiance to the world that fed them.

"Too late for glory, but in time for the locomotive, alas." So Alfred de Musset's generation saw their fate, and the railroad was the symbol of the Industrial Revolution. As Lewis Mumford has pointed out, productivity and ugliness advanced together in the age of coal and steam. Smoke fouled the air; industrial wastes polluted the water; and the earth was pockmarked with slag heaps. People left the countryside for new cities that sprang up near sources of cheap power and the cities, new and old, increased the world's ugliness. The very springs of life seemed troubled as the new factories offered women and children the chance to work exhaustingly long hours under brutalizingly unhealthful conditions. Furthermore, since women and children often were employable when their men were not, observers of the early phases of the Industrial Revolution prophesied an eroding of family ties and male domination.

At whatever cost, the economy grew as the Industrial Revolution spread from England to the United States and continental Europe during the nineteenth century. With that wealth came new wealth, new opportunities, new pressures, and new modes of achieving identity.

The Calvinist phase of the Protestant Revolt had opened the way; the Industrial Revolution required that the way be followed: an increasing number of individuals became aware of their identity in terms of identification with the social role of money maker. But success in that role meant adaptation to the ideal of the "economic man," a person who knew what his economic interests were and allowed nothing to interfere with the rational pursuit of his object: the largest possible profit in order to achieve the greatest possible accumulation. Free competition was recognized as the road to profit; the war of each against all was the economic rule of life. In this war, most men must accept defeat, of course. It is interesting to recall that it was from Thomas Malthus' attempt to convince opponents of the new social framework that they should realize that the framework could not be replaced with one more humane, that Darwin derived the inspiration for his theory of evolution and, from Darwin's theory, Herbert Spencer and his followers developed what Hofstadter has called "social Darwinism."

People multiply faster than food supplies, said Malthus; hence, chastity alone could permanently improve the lot of the Christian laboring man, for that would reduce his numbers and increase each man's share of a necessarily limited total. Darwin carried the Malthusian principle into the animal and vegetable worlds: physical modifications that improve a creature's competitive position in the struggle for a limited food supply can be passed on by heredity and so account for the changes that have occurred in species over the long course of time. And in the late nineteenth century the social Darwinists interpreted the struggle for profit as the road by which human society had evolved from the primitive regime of status to the regime of contract, which had emancipated the individual and filled the world with good things. According to this view, man was indeed a commodity but a commodity whose disposal he controlled. Thus, implicitly at least, identity was individuation primarily, and individuation appeared most clearly when the person was in economic conflict with all other persons, within the bounds that the law allowed.

This philosophy presents the alienated man as a kind of model. To other students of the nineteenth-century scene, however, *laissez faire* seemed no more than an assertion by the "haves" of their right to possession. Marx, one of the best-known social critics of his time and his society, declared that all social philosophies necessarily defended the right of the ruling class to rule, but no class had maintained itself in permanent power and the *bourgeoisie,* the latest successors to power, would ultimately, according to Marx, lose it to the proletariat, who would abolish all classes and begin a new era in human existence.

In twentieth-century America, the dynamism of the Industrial Revolution may seem a slow movement indeed. To nineteenth-century men, however, the changes they were experiencing seemed deplorably rapid. In the most important countries, industry replaced agriculture as the prevailing way of life. People left the closeness of village life for the increasing impersonality of life in great cities. Men stood faced by new problems of relating to themselves and to others, problems that the Church did little to resolve although it was the traditional institution of human understanding and charity. Darwin and his interpreters offered a more scientific understanding of man's place in the universe, but that merely confronted men with the need to establish their identity. Finally,

Freud provided essential clues by which men could understand their own bewildering selves. But Freud's insights, too, made it necessary for men to become aware of their identity in a new fashion.

Nevertheless, occupied as men were with the practical need to change social conditions and to acquire gradually the political power that would make improvements possible, only a few were aware that an identity crisis was developing during the nineteenth century. Because the family remained relatively stable, despite fuller education and greater economic opportunities for women, the traditional past seemed relevant, in Western Europe at least, and the superego could develop and maintain itself. In the United States, of course, and particularly in the immigrant household, tradition lost its relevance earlier and the family was somewhat less stable. There, too, technological change was more rapid and mobility, personal and social, more common. Hence the identity crisis may appear more sharply in this society than it does in Europe.

In summary, it is evident that different historical epochs are characterized by differences in identity both as seen from outside and as experienced from within. The changes in identity that took place during the Middle Ages, the great transition era of the Renaissance, the Reformation, and the Industrial Revolution all occurred over long, but decreasing, periods of time. Only a few unusually perceptive contemporaries were aware of what was happening as identity known through identification gave way to identity known through individuation. Modern man is less happily situated. More and more, he is consciously aware of identity as a problem of his own. Modern men have an image of a world far broader than that known to any men in the past. They feel the swift pace of technological change in their own skins, for automation threatens them with the unemployment of obsolescence and atomic armament threatens them with a new dimension of warfare. Even in affluent, high-consuming societies, men feel empty. T. S. Eliot wrote of the "hollow men" and urged that they fill the void by reviving the religious and political faiths of the past, an enterprise with minimal chance of success. A great modern sculptor surrounds space with the huge openings in the bodies of his human figures. And increasingly, the psychotherapist sees patients who ask not "Why can't I do what I want?" but "What do I want?" and "Who am I?"

And in those questions one finds modern man's awareness of his distinctive identity problem.

III. EXISTENCE AND IDENTITY

This chapter looks at identity and its problems in terms of contemporary philosophy and particularly of existentialism. For this philosophy is particularly relevant to problems involved in studying identity and the issues connected with its establishment and maintenance. Existentialism holds that existence precedes essence and that identity is bound up with existence. This may sound like a truism, but many significant philosophic and psychological insights do seem truisms at first sight. Where earlier philosophies have stressed the concept of essence, the existentialists emphasize that before man can be aware of himself as essence—as soul, spirit, intelligence, or the like—he must be aware of himself as an existent, a being present in the here-and-now. As a concept, *essence* refers to a universal past. To quote Hegel's untranslatable pun "wesen (essence) ist was gewesen ist" (what was). *Existence,* in contrast, refers to what is and is to be.

Since the concept of man's existence is not predetermined by concepts of essence, men are free to identify themselves with, and through, their existence. Existentialism became fashionable in the forties and fifties largely because it spoke more meaningfully than most philosophies to those who were dissatisfied and disenchanted with the situation of contemporary man and his society. As discovered, or more properly, rediscovered by the post-World War II generation, existentialism could be considered more than a new philosophy; rather it seemed a new mode of life and existence.

Nevertheless, the number of persons who really grasp the meaning and content of existentialist philosophy is distressingly small. Many have equated Sartre with the existentialist movement and often were not even aware of the provocative statements of Kierkegaard, who truly forecast the anxiety of our age. Too few persons still are really acquainted with Heidegger, who followed in the footsteps of Husserl and brought existentialism of age.

All contemporary existential philosophers from Jaspers to Marcel are concerned with the emptiness and nothingness with which modern life confronts us. They all are concerned by the loss of self, the dehumanization and depersonalization of people living in a technological society. All of them stress the fate of man faced with the struggle of his inner experiences. Compared with the situation in the nineteenth century, where only a few perceptive men saw where modern technological society was likely to lead those who lived in it, the existential dilemma has changed: Existential freedom, the recognition that we are finite and doomed, is no longer a right. It has become a contingency, the accidental outgrowth of a period's making and benefiting from some special encounter or experience.

Thus we see how closely existential philosophy approaches the problem of identity. Jean-Paul Sartre, saying "We are our choices," reflects one of the central aspects of the problem of identity. Modern man, faced with numerous choices and decisions, becomes so involved and identified with them that he may certainly be said to *be* them in something of Sartre's sense. We are, in other words, the manifestation of our personal choices and our choices and circumstances are a part of our being. Yet the creature who creates himself by making his choices has no choice about that which precedes both his power and his obligation to choose: man is "thrown" into the world, as Heidegger puts it. Nevertheless, man is totally identified with his existence and that existence, as shown in his choices, is his identity. Camus, for example, intimates in his *Mythe de Sisyphe* that a man must either make his choice and live by it or deny his very existence. This recalls Kierkegaard's old battle cry, the title of one of his best-known works, *Either/Or*. Unfortunately, in modern American society the man who wants to make his own choices and insists on his right to do so is often limited by societal circumstances, such as the emergence of large-scale organizations which all but dictate the external circumstances of most people's lives. Consequent inability to carry choices through, when and if choices are made, tends to imbue the individual with feelings of helplessness in the face of mass society. The man who cannot act in accord with Sartre's "We are our choices" is likely to intensify his anxiety and despair. Obviously, a man who cannot make the choices that are the foundations of his existence, or carry them out if he does make them, will find himself in trouble. A pattern of behavior emerges. Existence becomes a struggle to find the right choices or to avoid the necessity of making any choices at all. But a man who makes what he thinks are the right choices may well find himself criticized or even subjected to punishment by the society or organization of which he is a part. To refuse to make any choice at all is to be *nothing*,[1] yet even such a refusal is in

[1] The fear to be *nothing* or experience nothingness (that is, emptiness) seems to be one of the recurrent themes in our mass society today for the individual in search of an identity. Barbara Probst Solomon speaks in her essay "The Person Alone" (*Dissent*, Summer 1961) even of "Nothing life." Since nothingness in existential terms expresses itself

itself a choice. The man who makes that refusal often detaches himself from the responsibilities, duties, and obligations imposed on him by modern mass society. Thus, whether a man chooses consciously or unconsciously, or whether he refuses to make choices, trouble awaits him in the modern mass society. The man who makes a conscious choice that society disapproves often finds himself in a state of despair, dread, aloneness, and anxiety. But the man who abstains from choice or makes the nonchoice which is, of course, a major act of choosing, may end in the same dark condition.

It is surprising that American philosophers have not more fully investigated the preoccupation with anxiety, despair, dread, aloneness, and guilt in their society. The obvious relationship between the existential concept of man's involvement with his existence and with the problems which are a part of that existence have yet to be fully analyzed in terms of modern American society. If we take certain disquieting characteristics of human life in the mass society one by one, we may underline how broadly the current existential situation affects and determines identity.

The problem of aloneness in our society is obvious not only to sociologists and psychologists but also to perceptive laymen. We should, of course, distinguish between aloneness and loneliness. The solitary man is not necessarily unhappy or in despair. Aloneness and loneliness do go hand in hand in numerous instances, however, and for the moment I shall ignore the distinction. Concentration of people certainly does not lessen loneliness, for it is precisely in large cities where life is truly anonymous that loneliness seems most prevalent. It is in mass society that man is most alone. Although organizations of every kind flourish and people come together and share interests, they seem to feel no less alone. That the aged, the chronically sick, and the poor should be forgotten by all but impersonal relief agencies might not be wondered at. That men and women in early adult life should feel forgotten, cast off and cast out when their office doors close behind them—this may seem strange to those who have not walked what Margaret Mary Wood calls "the paths of loneliness." Yet we need only look at the New York evening papers each week end to see how great the need is to cope with loneliness and how considerable the profit in offering to meet that need.

in aloneness and loneliness, one might also have a look at two interesting and challenging papers on this subject: H. D. von Witzleben "On Loneliness," *Psychiatry*, Vol. 21, 37, and N. W. Winnicott, "The Capacity to be Alone," *Int. Journal of Psychoanalysis*, Vol. 39, 416.

Perhaps the "lonely hearts" are the price we pay for the growth of metropolitan centers.

In "The Person Alone," Barbara Probst Solomon gives a penetrating description of the person living alone in New York, but her observations certainly apply to other metropolitan centers in American society. Although this essay deals with the unmarried person particularly, certain of her observations could probably be applied to married people as well.

The loneliness that authors such as those just cited have portrayed is closely linked to two other aspects of current distress, isolation and the inability to communicate. Mass communication is essential to our world, but increasingly, people as individuals seem unable either to talk to or to listen to each other.[2] Yet communication is essential to any genuine participation in the social world. That advertisers, politicians, and other public figures should use a singularly opaque verbal medium may be understandable, for these are professional persons schooled in the theorem that words are our principal means of concealing thought. But it seems more and more difficult for people to share their problems in any genuinely helpful way.

Out of this situation grows the increasing role of the professional counselor, ranging all the way from the tea-leaf reader, who now has "Advisor" painted on the window of her tawdry store-front office, and the newspaper columnist, to the trained psychotherapist. People want and need advice; they are so involved in their own problems that they cannot see their situation objectively and they are no longer able to communicate with close relatives or friends. Consequently, troubled persons turn elsewhere for support in their conscious choices. In most cases, to be sure, those who seek advice merely want the choices they have actually made to be sustained and confirmed. Hence, the heavy correspondence that reaches the desks of the marriage counselors of the women's magazines, for example, or the psychologists' columns carried by many newspapers. Thousands of persons write to the authors of these columns, persons who cannot share their problems with those in their immediate environment and who want to be told that they are making the right choice. Often enough the advice received is ignored, because the questioner had already made his (or more often her) decision and sought only sustaining and comforting approval. If the advice runs contrary to that decision already perhaps only half-consciously reached, then the counsel will be

[2] For some interesting views on the "vocabulary of culture" and American culture in particular, see *The Silent Language* by Edward T. Hall (New York: Doubleday, 1959; Premierbooks, 1961).

rejected. It is the act of seeking advice and reassurance that is important. For the seeker wants human contact rather than the benefit of human wisdom.

Desire to communicate and establish contact and so escape the burden of isolation seems to grow as ability to communicate diminishes. This is brought out poignantly in Edward Albee's *The Zoo Story*, in which a young man who lives alone in a West Side rooming house tells how he so longed for contact with some living creature that he tried to make friends with his janitor's dog. "We regard each other with a mixture of sadness and suspicion, and then we feign indifference," he says. "We walk past each other safely; we have an understanding. It's very sad, but you'll have to admit that it is an understanding. We had made many attempts at contact, and we failed."[3]

Enmeshed in such depths of aloneness, the person feels isolated. If his strength (or his passivity) is sufficient, he may make isolation part of his identity pattern. Indeed, many persons are coming to accept isolation as the price they must pay for being a part of this society. Isolation is a major theme in current American literature, as Edwin Bowden points out in *The Dungeon of the Human Heart*. Isolation has also been a strong theme in the other arts, such as painting, sculpture, and the theater.

Perhaps it is peculiarly congruent to the mass society that the individual should feel not only isolated but also insignificant, a cog in a huge machine. Life in a mass society may tend to accelerate the decline of both the individual and his society. For the health of a society may be measured by the degree to which a person can distinguish himself from others. When he cannot make this distinction confidently, he ceases to be able to function as a fully individuated person. He may withdraw from many aspects of living and then come to experience a feeling of loneliness even though he continues to be part of a family, active in associations, or involved in other forms of organized behavior in society.

Obviously, the problems of aloneness and loneliness did not originate with our industrial mass society; they are as old as human history. But the loneliness and aloneness experienced in the past were of quite another kind. Thus, in the eighteenth and nineteenth centuries, such poets as Goethe, Hölderlin, Heine, and Rilke romanticized loneliness; musicians such as Schubert made it actual in such compositions as "Die Schöne Müllerin" and "Die Winterreise." Loneliness may have been

[3] Edward Albee, *The Zoo Story* (New York: Coward-McCann, Inc., 1960), p. 43.

a sad experience in the pre-industrial world but it was not drably grim as loneliness has become in our time.[4]

It is during periods of transition, such as the decades since the First World War, that loneliness has become a societal problem. One need only look at European literature during the 1920's and at the writings of Franz Kafka in particular to see the supreme expression of the loneliness of the individual who feels himself totally insignificant, desolate, and alone. In *The Trial, The Castle,* and most of all in the terrifying story, "The Metamorphosis," Kafka portrays the type of loneliness that seems characteristic of such a period of transition. Even in Kafka's Prague, the Industrial Revolution and the growth of the capitalist system had produced an immense bureaucracy, which greatly contributed to the individual's sense of meaninglessness and insignificance. Twenty years later, Camus' *The Stranger* shows a similar picture: man alone in a meaningless world over which he could exert no fruitful control.

Aloneness and loneliness are expressed in many other ways in our society, for they constitute a problem closely connected with both the identity and the existence of modern man. Loneliness and inability to communicate create situations in which people find it peculiarly difficult to maintain satisfactory relations with their fellows. Difficulties in this area tend to produce anxiety and under the pressure of anxiety, breakdowns in personal relationships occur and give rise to a multitude of problems, individual and social.

Among adults, divorce, crime, mental illness, or general psychological insecurity give evidence of a breakdown of ability to maintain satisfactory human relationships. Among adolescents, juvenile delinquency is an evident kind of breakdown in human relationships, but the general growth of concern about adolescents and their problems shows how widespread is the breakdown of relationships both among individuals and between individuals and society.

Fifty years ago the adolescent was often considered funny and adolescence was looked upon as a peculiarly amusing stage in human development. Something of this attitude may still linger in the tone of tolerant exasperation that often still marks social attitudes toward "teenagers," but it scarcely seems conceivable that such a book as Booth Tarkington's *Seventeen* would become a best seller in the 1960's. Today, adolescence seems to be considered less a normal phase of human development than a special problem, almost indeed a

---

[4] Elements of contemporary loneliness are very well described in David Riesman's essay "The Suburban Sadness," in *Suburbia,* ed. William Dobriner (New York: G. P. Putnam's Sons, 1958).

threat. The psychoanalytically oriented sociologist might see in this a kind of obverse of the Oedipus complex: rather than the son's fearing punishment by the father, the father fears an accusation by the son; the older generation fears that adolescents are sufficiently in rebellion against adult values to endanger the future of those values.

More striking than breakdowns in relationships between adolescents and adults are the symptoms of breakdown in relationships between adults and children. One need only read Erik Erikson's perceptive *Childhood and Society* to know how much the child in our time has become a problem to himself and his parents. During the eighteenth and nineteenth centuries a paradigm of innocence, the child in our time, like the adolescent, has become a "problem." One need only mention the numerous special schools and institutions that have been founded in the last twenty or thirty years in order to care for children who are unable to function satisfactorily in relation to the world around them. In *Love Is Not Enough* and *Truants from Life,* Bruno Bettelheim has shown the frightful desolation of the modern child.[5] But the strain is not upon the child alone; the parent, and particularly the middle-class parent who sets the tone for our society, experiences a tension at least partly derived from his education and his conscientious concern to help his child achieve a problematic "good life."

The breakdown just described as resulting from aloneness and loneliness, from the felt separation among individuals and between those individuals and their society, shows that a probably increasing number of persons are unable to communicate satisfactorily with their environment. They have suffered depletion and even loss of identity both in the sense of identification (which requires communication and stability) and in the sense of individuation (which requires opportunity for the person to maintain himself as an independent being). Such breakdown in the awareness and exercise of identity also involves a breakdown in the person's relation to existence, in the philosophic sense. Hence, unless the very roots of a patient's existence are analyzed, it is impossible for him to resolve his identity crisis.

Another aspect of the relationship between philosophical existentialism and identity problems, for example, is the characteristic preoccupation, of American society, with death,

[5] Bruno Bettelheim, *Love Is Not Enough* (New York: The Free Press of Glencoe, 1950), and *Paul and Mary* (New York: Doubleday Anchor, 1961); this paperback presents part of *Truants from Life.* See also Melanie Klein, *The Psychoanalysis of Children* (New York: Grove Press, 1960).

despair, dread, and anxiety. In Chapter I, individual neurotic anxiety was distinguished from the anxiety which men share as social beings and as human persons continuously confronted with existence itself. Here it seems necessary to go beyond the existential anxiety which is peculiarly hard to endure in transitional societies like our own and to consider three other aspects of the relationship between identity and existence, namely, despair, dread, and death. Philosophers have long been occupied with all three, of course, but the quality of our current preoccupation seems different.

Despair and dread have become the concern of contemporary philosophers, as the works of Heidegger, Sartre, and Jaspers all show, and are always linked with death in their writings. Heidegger is as much concerned with death as he is with dread since in his opinion the very essence of dread is, precisely, dread of death. Here we approach the realm of psychology and psychoanalysis which teach us that man's fear or dread is essentially fear of death—of failure to survive.

Thus Jaspers can say, "Philosophieren heiszt sterben lernen,"[6] "to philosophize means to learn how to die." The existentialist considers death not as something beyond life, but as the last stage of life, as one in the series of events termed life and a present existential reality.

Sartre has said, "Man can only meet what is human," but death is a human phenomenon, the ultimate phenomenon of life, part of life. As such it influences the whole life, as a counter-current.[7]

Once it could be contended that Americans were deeply concerned with huddling the fact of death out of sight, but this can no longer be considered to be true. Rather, Americans, like other people, seem to have taken account of Freud's observation that modern man would do well if he learned that he was living beyond his psychological means and prepared for death in order to be better able to endure life.[8] In a world where life expectancy has been prolonged, where respect for life—Bergen-Belsen and Dachau notwithstanding—has taken on new meaning and dimensions, existential philosophers are still concerned with death.[9]

6 Quoted from I. M. Bochenski, *Europäische Philosophie der Gegenwart* (Bern: 1947), p. 198. See also the English translation of this book published by University of California Press, 1961, paperback edition, p. 197.

7 Jean-Paul Sartre, *Being and Nothingness* (New York: Philosophical Library, 1956), p. 616.

8 Sigmund Freud, "Thoughts for the Times on War and Death," *Collected Papers* (London: Hogarth Press, 1956), Vol. IV, pp. 316-17.

9 See Herman Feifel, ed., *The Meaning of Death* (New York: McGraw-Hill Book Co., 1959) and "Death—Relevant Variable in Psy-

And in a country that worships youth and, presumably, life, death seems a constant presence. In *The Loved One*, Evelyn Waugh paints a brilliantly satiric picture of the way in which death is brought into the orbit of American business. In reading this book, I recalled my own somewhat shocked surprise at my first sight of a neon sign on a "funeral home." The squeamish emphasis on the function of the undertaker (Latinized to the elegant "mortician") seems almost macabre. Although extravagant spending on funerals is common in many countries, the amounts spent in America seem even more disproportionate. In a peculiar way, these expenditures are related to the desire to remain young, or at least to give the appearance of youth. Except for extremely orthodox Jews and a few other old-fashioned people, hardly anyone is buried in a shroud. The dead are laid in silk-lined coffins, clad in their best, curled and painted, not simply to cover the fact of death but to give the appearance of youth. For in the United States everyone wants to stay "sweet and twenty" or, at least, handsome and thirty.

Beauty parlors, health studios, gymnasiums flourish. Not only women, who are traditionally supposed to be susceptible to the dictates of fashions in sexual attraction, but men starve themselves in the midst of plenty in order to preserve a youthful appearance. People conceal their ages and seem reluctant even to admit that the years pass and leave their traces. Fewer and fewer little old wrinkled grandmothers are to be seen, although there are numbers of "middle-aged" women with carefully tended skins and hair, and transparent nylon stockings thinly covering elderly legs. In short, preserving and prolonging life and youth are all-important. One is reminded of the small boy who wanted to be Peter Pan because, staying young forever, Peter would never die.

It is not without significance that America is the home of Christian Science, which denies that pain or death is real, and of the world's most advanced geriatric medicine. And all these—the gilding of death, the clutching at youth, the denial of actuality—paradoxically set death and the fear of dying at the center of the modern American's existence even when he is, or claims to be, wholly unaware of the situation.

In summary, such aspects of existence and identity as loneliness, aloneness, death, despair, dread, and anxiety are not in themselves philosophical concerns: they have become so because of the situation of man in modern society. These phenomena are not new in themselves. One need only read

chology," *Existential Philosophy*, ed. Rollo May (New York: Random House, 1961).

Kierkegaard to find an analysis of them in the nineteenth century: but loneliness, death, despair, dread, and anxiety have emerged more sharply and bulk larger in our modern mass society. Philosophical problems have become social and psychological problems; the philosopher can no longer be detached from the world. As Jaspers says, he is "being-in-the-world." For this reason, it is interesting to consider the sociological aspects of existentialism in connection with the establishing and maintenance of identity.

Except for Ernst Topitsch's very interesting essay, "The Sociology of Existentialism," we have few significant sociological studies of existentialism.[10] Topitsch believes that existentialism can be traced back through the centuries. He also holds that one of the most interesting aspects of existential philosophy is its relationship between the problems of knowledge and the problems of value. Topitsch notes that the language of every day refuses to separate knowledge from values, but rather recognizes values as "properties" of phenomena. When social tensions and conflicts make values fluid, however, crises become more and more common. "In such periods of convulsion, people often turn to philosophy in order to win back their lost *security* [my italics], and they are then ready to pay for it every price, even that of intellectual integrity."

When we consider existential philosophy in terms of the crisis of our times, we can see how it is related to the desire to regain, in Topitsch's phrase, *lost security*.[11] For each aspect of the relation of existence and identity: death, despair, loneliness, and anxiety—represents the loss of security man formerly enjoyed. Man in America has had to pay with loss of security for increased affluence, better living conditions, a longer life, more leisure, and all other advantages of modern society. The other-directed man has replaced the secure inner-directed man, to use Riesman's terms once again.

The relation between existential philosophy and the identity crisis experienced in mass society is self-evident. No other philosophy has penetrated the problems of man's existence, which *is* his identity, as successfully. For only existentialism declares, as in *Waiting for Godot* Vladimir and Estragon say it, in the following words:

Vladimir: You are right, we're inexhaustible.
Estragon: It's so we won't think.
Vladimir: We have that excuse.

10 *Partisan Review*, May-June, 1954.
11 *Ibid.*, pp. 291-292.

Estragon: It's so we won't hear.
Vladimir: We have our reasons.
Estragon: All the dead voices.
Vladimir: They make a noise like wings.
Estragon: Like leaves.
Vladimir: Like sand.
Estragon: Like leaves.[12]

Of all the existentialist thinkers, Camus seems to be the most positive in outlook in saying, "Nevertheless, I do not believe there is no responsibility in the world." Here Camus comes close to Buber's "In the beginning is relation" which puts him squarely in the field of the social psychologists. Buber listens to existence and he waits for something other than an echo of the "I." Camus also believes that the relation with others is essential for a continuous sense of the self. To live defiantly or to create dangerously does not mean nihilism. "I am tired of nihilism," he said in one of his last lectures. And so in Camus' world there is still hope for man to be man, for the individual to achieve his full identity.

IV. PSYCHOANALYSIS AND IDENTITY

Sigmund Freud presented the earliest, the most complete, and the most dynamic theory of personality, in his psycho-analytic approach to man. Freud's theory of personality and Freudian psychoanalysis have had a great influence in America and one which is still increasing.[1] Not only have Freud's theories affected the specific theories of personality developed by American sociologists, anthropologists, and social psychologists, but psychoanalysis has, so to speak, infiltrated the social sciences in general. This development has been particularly marked in the last two decades. Nor is interest in psychoanalysis confined to professional circles, for it has acquired widespread popular appeal: so much so that we may almost

---

[12] Samuel Beckett, *Waiting for Godot* (New York: Grove Press, 1954), pp. 62-63.

[1] Although there is no current sociological study on the impact of Freudian thinking in America, there are numerous observations on the influence of psychoanalysis on the social sciences. See especially Harold Lasswell's essay, "The Impact of Psychoanalytic Thinking on the Social Sciences" in *The State of the Social Sciences*, Leonard D. White, ed. (Chicago: U. of Chicago Press, 1956), p. 84. This essay also appears in *Psychoanalysis and Social Science*, Hendrik M. Ruitenbeek, ed. (New York: Dutton Everyman Paperbacks, 1962). In this volume, see also "Psychoanalysis: A Challenge to the Social Sciences."

speak with John R. Seeley of "the Americanization of the unconscious."[2] Indeed, Freud's theories were accepted and applied in America (particularly in the field of the social sciences) before they became respectable in Europe. This is not too surprising when one realizes the opportunities offered by a highly mobile and rapidly changing society. In such a society, however, the individual tends to become less secure than a similar individual in a social structure that is less affected by change. Insecurity may tend to make individuals somewhat more receptive to new ideas about the development of personality and its problems than those in a rigid society from which they may get greater support.

This chapter will not summarize the whole range of personality theories in America, although the significance of the work of Clyde Kluckhohn, Abram Kardiner, Margaret Mead, Ralph Linton, and Edward Sapir, to name only a few workers in this field, should be understood.[3] Nor shall we discuss the aspects of social character that have been brought to the fore in recent years through the work of Erich Fromm and David Riesman. Rather, we shall try to bring into perspective the psychoanalytic aspects of the study of personality with particular reference to the concept of identity. More specifically, this chapter tries to trace the relationship between the psychoanalytic view of personality and the concept of the identity crisis. Have there, in short, been any changes in psychoanalytic theory and practice which tend to show that identity has become a crucial problem for contemporary American patients in psychoanalysis?

Let us first sketch the scope and impact of psychoanalysis in this country. General and clinical psychology has enormous influence in medicine, in the social sciences, and in education, to name only three fields. Psychoanalysis as a specific phase of therapy has become increasingly important and is genuinely accepted. Many persons are even self-conscious about the psychoanalytic implications of their actions. Even more are familiar with general psychological terminology. In distorted version, psychological and psychoanalytic terms have entered popular usage. Almost everybody knows what an "inferiority

[2] The Atlantic Monthly, July, 1961, p. 68. Also in Hendrik M. Ruitenbeek, ed., op. cit.

[3] See Personality in Nature, Society, and Culture, ed. Clyde Kluckhohn et al. (New York: Alfred A Knopf, 1959); Clyde Kluckhohn, Mirror for Man (New York: Premierbooks, 1960); Abram Kardiner, The Psychological Frontiers of Society (New York: Columbia University Press, 1945); Abram Kardiner, The Individual and His Society (New York: Columbia University Press, 1939; New York: Mentor Books, 1950); Edward Sapir, Culture, Language and Personality (Berkeley, Calif.: University of California Press, 1956).

complex" is supposed to be, and the Oedipus conflict is sufficiently familiar to supply material for jokes that are well received by night-club audiences.

Psychotherapy and psychoanalysis are approved not only by intellectuals and academicians, but by the middle class as a whole. Psychoanalysis is not only a respected therapy, but has even become fashionable. "Being in analysis" almost ranks as a status symbol among certain groups of Americans. So general an acceptance of psychoanalysis points toward the widespread need for psychological help that individuals in our society have come to feel.

Then, we see that psychoanalysis has affected American thinking both as an influence on social scientists and as therapy to which the prosperous and influential tend to resort. Since the early 1900's, when Freud's ideas first began to become known, psychoanalytic insights have filtered down and become a permanent part of the thinking and behavior of American society.

Many examples of this penetration might be cited. Many Americans no longer take anything at its face value. Everything must have some inner meaning; everything, even the most idle remarks, must be interpreted. We have gone far beyond merely regarding slips of the tongue as "Freudian," and have become self-conscious about our most ordinary behavior. This self-consciousness may well contribute to anxiety and insecurity. Many a person is just sufficiently well acquainted with psychoanalytic thinking to know that what he says, and even what gestures he may make, can betray his "unconscious motives" to the alert and informed observer. Such a person, perhaps himself willing to jump at conclusions about others, may feel acutely aware that others are watching and appraising him in the light of their psychoanalytic knowledge, though that may be as scanty as his own. He feels vulnerable, is often unable to relax in the company of others, and suffers under the pressure of constraint.

Even children are aware of the penetration of psychoanalytic thought into the adult world. Some of this awareness arises from the impact that psychoanalysis has had on educational theory and practice. To quote from John R. Seeley:

"The role of teacher as a parent surrogate is understood and accepted. It is expected that hostility will be displaced upon her, that drawings, essays, polite exchanges have covert meanings, much different from their overt content—and much more real and much more interesting. The libidinal give-and-take that accompanies all communications (or motivates it?) is noted, although less easily accepted.

"If Johnny throws a spitball at Mary, nothing so ordinary

as mischief is afoot. The possibilities have to be—are joy-ously—entertained that Johnny is working off aggression, compensating for deeply felt inferiority, asserting his masculinity in ways appropriate to his developmental stage, testing for limits, or, in a characteristic upside-down way, saying to Mary in a circuitous and hence safe way, 'I love you.' "[4]

Even more of the child's awareness of psychoanalytic influence is rooted in the peculiar situation in which the American child finds himself. To Europeans, American children have long seemed offensively precocious, at once too much the object of adult attention and too little the object of adult discipline. These trends, which are deeply rooted in the American past, have become even more conspicuous in our own time as Americans are more aware of themselves and their behavior, and as American society speeds on in its technological growth. Occasionally one even gets the somewhat frightening thought that American children are not children at all, but are small adults, with all the rather unfortunate consequences of this type of behavior. Children in America seem to be taken with a far greater degree of seriousness and society gives them far more importance than it does in Europe. Because American society is more fluid than European, children are the educators as well as the educated. So it is possible for Riesman to observe that, in the United States, children train their parents in the ways of the other-directed society. Eric H. Larrabee remarks that childhood in America "is a self-perpetuating subculture with a remarkable degree of integrity, and an even more remarkable effectiveness in preparing its members for the primary conflicts of their later lives."[5] One may well dispute the effectiveness of their preparation when one considers the adult world, afflicted as it is by a high divorce rate, sexual deviation, mental illness, crime, and the frequent lack of direction among individuals. Nevertheless, the subculture of childhood, and particularly the subculture of adolescence—the highly institutionalized world of the teenager, so profitable to purveyors of merchandise—is sufficiently real to create problems of its own. The psychotherapist sees many disturbed children and perhaps even more disturbed or confused adolescents. Some of these distresses and confusions arise from disturbances in the family situation, of course, but others are derived from the adult culture and from the subculture that is the American child's world.

    [4] *The Atlantic Monthly*, July, 1961, p. 72.
    [5] *The Self-Conscious Society* (New York: Doubleday & Co., 1960), p. 132.

Child training, as Larrabee observes, "is an expression of culture,"[6] but often the American culture in its contemporary form seems to feed on as much as to nurture its children. Again to quote Larrabee, "Childhood is something which American adults experience vicariously."[7] Perhaps because the culture seems increasingly to push the child forward to assuming at least the mask of adult behavior, adults seek to live out the childhoods of which they feel cheated by observing and recording children's behavior. One might well argue that the training that American culture gives to its children is inadequate because it has nothing to do with the world of adults. Because the American child so rarely gets the opportunity to live as a child his primary conflicts remain unresolved and even unrecognized. Perhaps this eclipse of childhood in a world that is called *child-centered* helps account for the difficulty so many have in establishing a sense of identity sufficient to help them accept the responsibilities, restrictions, and opportunities of adulthood.

As has been said, the peculiar experience of the American child, and especially of the middle-class child who is most likely to come into analysis, tends to make difficult the establishment of identity. The therapist is tempted to suspect that many patients do not enter analysis in order to get the analyst to unveil some difficult and complex problem, but in order to find a point of security. For persons like those whom Lillian Ross has been describing in her *New Yorker* stories (characters who bear a marked resemblance to contemporary human beings),[8] psychoanalysis has become an accepted way to assert identity. Once in analysis, a patient can say he is "doing something about" the problem of his identity and his existence. Security, to be sure, is essential if people are to function in society. In many instances, analysis provides at least a fancied security for the patient who finds in his analyst the genuinely listening ear, which no other relationship in his life provides.

As has been pointed out earlier, many persons seek analytic treatment with no clear ideas about what ails them. Their problems are not embodied in physical symptoms: the analyst sees few hysteric patients, for example, although psychosomatic complaints are not uncommon. Often patients' problems are not even reflected in psychological disturbances, such as unhappy relationships or inability to work. To all appearances, patients may be the product of a well-balanced *ideal*

6 *Ibid.*, p. 122.
7 *Ibid.*, p. 120.
8 See, for example, "The Ordeal of Dr. Blauberman," *The New Yorker,* May 13, 1951, pp. 39–88.

American family, moving in a well-adjusted group of persons and outwardly leading well-adjusted and economically productive lives.

Yet those lives seem without real meaning to those who are living them. When those who have enjoyed and do enjoy the advantages of the favored sectors of society—economic well-being, good homes, adequate education, status-conferring vocations, opportunities for sexual fulfillment—find themselves lonely, insecure, and anxious, and when such experience is common, the psychoanalyst must recognize that he faces a cultural situation as well as an individual problem. Whether he be Freudian, Jungian, Frommian, or Sullivanian in outlook, the contemporary analyst must take the patient's cultural context into consideration. Analytic ideologies, programs, and techniques must be revised in order to take account of, and cope with, the changing social picture.

Often it seems that the clinician does not adequately realize the importance of the social implications of the patient's problems; the analyst is not sufficiently attentive to the sociocultural background of his patients and their situations. Consequently, analysis can become an obsessive activity for patients hopelessly and helplessly searching for help in resolving their ill-defined or undefined problems. In their separate ways, stories like those of Lillian Ross and disguised autobiographies like *The Frog Pond* by "Joyce McIver" describe the desperation of patients searching in analysis for an identity that their culture has given them so little help in building for themselves.

If we agree that modern man is experiencing an identity crisis, and if, further, we recognize that individuals turn to psychoanalysis for help in meeting their crisis, we must consider the function of analysis in such a context. First, the analyst must be fully acquainted with the society in which he and his patients live. Only then can he appreciate the predicament of a patient who is beset by his own version of the identity problem. Yet the analyst cannot lose sight of the limitations of his own activity. Psychoanalysis cannot give a patient a new identity; it can only make him more aware of his thoughts and his feelings, and so free him to sense his lack of identity and in that freedom strengthen him in the effort to search for that aspect of his identity in which he knows and feels himself as a human being independent of tradition, parents, family, and friends.

Here, it seems appropriate to take account of some of the new light that existential psychology and existential psychoanalysis can cast upon the problems of identity and personality. Existential psychoanalysis is a recent growth in the United

States, although it has been a significant school in Europe for some time. Paul Tillich and Rollo May, who have been particularly influential in introducing existential psychoanalysis in the United States, have emphasized its relationship to insecurity, despair, and anxiety, the emotional roots of the problems that trouble men in modern society. Tillich's well-known book, *The Courage to Be,* and May's work as the editor of *Existence* have been particularly important in opening the minds of both analysts and laymen to the significance of existential psychoanalysis.[9]

The existential analyst is concerned with the patient's *total* existence. By definition, therefore, the existential analyst is concerned with the interrelationship between society and the patient. R. D. Laing, the English existential psychiatrist, has emphasized how important it is for the therapist to place himself in the framework of the patient's existence. Laing writes: ". . . every aspect of what he [the patient] is, is related in some ways to every other aspect, although the manner in which these aspects are articulated may be by no means clear. It is the task of existential phenomenology to articulate what the other's 'world' is and his way of being in it."[10]

Existentialists stress the immediacy of any human situation or encounter; hence it is obvious that only in the experience of that immediacy can the individual assert his identity in a day-to-day unique experience. Identity is not to be achieved by the patient's sitting back and talking to himself *out* to the analyst. Rather, it is a matter of beginning to realize what the "I" (which is Me) can do and has the potentiality to do. This realization implies growth, but growth that is visible and most exciting to patient and analyst.

Growth and search for identity is not necessarily confined to the relationship of analyst and patient, incidentally. In a broader context it takes place between persons in our society, when they begin to become conscious of their potentialities and to accept and realize the fact that choices and decisions are still there for them to take and make. Certainly the organizational society has tried (and in many instances has succeeded) to *depersonize* and dehumanize individuals, but those

9 Some recent publications on existential analysis might interest the reader. Although *Existence,* Rollo May *et al.,* eds. (New York: Basic Books, 1958) is an excellent sourcebook, it is not really intended for the lay readers. *Existential Psychology,* also edited by Rollo May, and published as a paperback by Random House (1961), is much simpler but far too short. *Psychoanalysis and Existential Philosophy,* Hendrik M. Ruitenbeek, ed. (New York: Dutton Everyman Paperbacks, 1962) is a collection of informative papers on existential analysis.

10 *The Divided Self, An Existential Study in Sanity and Madness* (Chicago: Quadrangle Books, 1960), p. 24.

who become aware of this should be better able to do something about it.

It is here that the immediacy of the existential school is relevant. This does not denigrate the significance of Freudian theory. In interpreting the dynamics of the patient's situation, an analyst cannot ignore the fundamental principles of Freudian theory. But the awareness of the patient that he is a part of the encounter and is growing in that experience, that is, is finding and asserting his unique identity, has become a major tool of the contemporary analyst to help his patient in establishing himself as a human person.

The patient who is struggling with specific identity problems has become familiar to the contemporary analyst. The contemporary patient, and for that matter men generally, do find it difficult to define their problems and often speak of them in terms of general aimlessness. Yet, many analysts have not realized the full significance of the clinical picture which patients are currently presenting. Traditional therapy does not provide the patient with immediate solutions and the patient has to wait it out, so to speak, and be patient. The identity crisis that faces the contemporary individual, however, does not allow him the luxury of taking it easy and working at his problem in a relaxed way. Identity problems such as role problems, goals, expectancy situations, require the immediate attention of the person involved; he does not have time for much contemplation. In the here-and-now situation, the individual must decide and it is he alone who must make the decision.

In contemporary mass society, however, individuals have not been reared along lines that develop their powers of choice and independence. This situation is responsible for many current identity problems and crises. Out of such crises, too, there develops the need for psychoanalytic treatment. As Thomas Szasz has pointed out, the purpose of psychoanalysis in general is *not* to socialize personality, but to enrich it with greater understanding and with responsibility for choice.[11]

It is on the point of the importance of socialization of personality that many psychoanalysts reject the premises of group therapy. For patients reared in a society such as ours, group therapy is not the treatment of choice for it does not deal effectively with the problem of the loss of and search for identity. Modern men are overly and perhaps falsely socialized at the expense of individual growth and development from within. A sense of identity cannot be achieved in group therapy because patients in group therapy cannot adequately

[11] *The New York Times Book Review*, May 14, 1961, p. 7.

develop new ways of looking at themselves, rather than at others. Hence, they are almost bound to remain entangled in the same type of problems that brought them to group therapy in the first place. In group therapy, the patient finds precisely the problem he must face in daily life, and he must listen to all the problems of his fellow-patients, irrelevant and trivial though they may seem.[12] A second objection to group therapy is less concerned with its relationship to the identity problem than to its being considered a kind of second best for the patient who cannot afford individual analysis. The patient does not, in other words, always seek group treatment out of a belief in its merits.

Only in the context of individual analysis can patients with identity problems find and learn to know themselves and then to achieve autonomy. But autonomy is not a goal that seems desirable to all patients. Szasz declares that "the make-believe companionship and disguised guidance"[13] which numbers of patients find in group therapy gives them a satisfaction akin to what the traditional Western faiths supplied once and, for many persons, apparently supply no longer.

Yet even in individual analysis, treatment of patients with identity problems requires that the analyst acquire a new, more sociological orientation. Personality theory oriented exclusively toward psychological and psychoanalytic concepts cannot serve adequately in a world where stable social values are more and more shaken by the pace of social change. The analyst whose patients feel unable to make truly independent choices, particularly where crucial goals are concerned, must be as familiar with the societal pressures upon them as he is with the psychodynamics of personality growth. For personality develops in the family context and families exist in the framework of society. Wheelis points out that as Freud and his contemporaries began the practice of psychoanalysis, they could validly assume the presence of stable social values, indeed of the nineteenth-century scientific and humanistic values with which they were all imbued. The contemporary analyst cannot make this assumption.[14] For many past value-systems are obsolete and no new ones have developed sufficiently powerful emotional roots to serve as

---

[12] An enlightening and informative defense of group psychotherapy may be found in Hyman Spotnitz, *The Couch and the Circle* (New York: Alfred A. Knopf, 1961).

[13] Thomas Szasz, *op. cit.*

[14] Allen Wheelis, in *The Quest for Identity* (New York: W. W. Norton & Co., 1958), has made an attempt to fictionalize the experience of the individual in search for identity. But the characterization is not vivid enough for the book to strike the reader as embodying a real and individual experience.

a basis for the easy and unconscious growth of individual identity.

One objective of psychoanalysis is freeing the individual to the point where he can make independent choices, where he can direct his life in freedom from neurotic compulsions. The analyst cannot do this without concern with, and understanding of, the objectives and current ideologies of the societal structure. Only the analyst who understands the cultural dynamics of society, can effectively communicate with and help his patients.

Here it should be fairly obvious that of the present schools of psychoanalysis, the existential group comes nearest to the needs of the contemporary patient, but even its practitioners often lack adequate cultural and sociological understanding. As far as the other psychotherapeutic schools are concerned, the followers of Horney, Sullivan, and Fromm tend to put too much emphasis on group therapy and interpersonal relationships to be able to help patients to establish a new sense of individual identity. The Freudian school, however orthodox it may be, has more likelihood of being able to adapt itself to taking account of the sociological and cultural variables with which the analyst must be familiar if he is to approach his patient in terms of the society of the twentieth century and not of the nineteenth.

In terms of techniques, we may expect treatment to remain much the same as it has been. But in terms of the approach, attitude, and philosophy of the analyst himself, great changes must be made if psychoanalysis is to continue its development. These changes may invalidate some of Freud's basic assumptions. It may well be that there is room for a completely new approach in terms of cultural and sociological dynamics as well as for further development within the Existential and Freudian schools.

The discussion of the identity problem in terms of specific psychoanalytic treatments and methods is only just beginning. In the coming decade, new ideas and methods will no doubt be developed in order to cope with the problem of identity faced by persons in our society.

V.   CHARACTER AND IDENTITY

The concept of social character has proved highly useful in the sociological interpretation of modern mass society. Social scientists often treat social character and identity as though they were synonymous, but I prefer to distinguish between the two, as this chapter will develop. For in this chapter we shall examine some of the content of American social character in its relation to the concept of identity.

During the last twenty years, four scholars have made significant contributions to our knowledge of social character. Margaret Mead has approached the problem from the anthropologist's point of view.[1] She holds that people in different societies express character traits in forms shaped by the ethos, the distinctive style of life of those societies, and particularly by the ways in which these societies develop their social concepts of the roles proper to child, woman, and man. In *Childhood and Society*, Erik H. Erikson has further developed the idea of social character as that which is seen by the psychoanalyst.[2] David Riesman and Erich Fromm have dealt with social character from a more strictly sociological point of view. In *The Lonely Crowd*, Riesman presents a general analysis of American society in terms of social character. He sees that character as an extension of individual personality and distinguishes between personality and character only where character is related to social forms. In other words, Riesman deals with "those components of character that are shared among significant social groups."[3]

Clearly, Riesman's definition of social character reflects his neo-Freudian convictions. Even in psychology, the neo-Freudian group stresses the role of the environment rather than of the instinctual drives of the individual. Thus they are led, in a sense, to emphasize the importance of the group rather than the individual in the study of society. Fromm goes further and makes the functioning of society a more important factor in shaping social character than is the character of the individuals in that society.[4] A society functions as historical and economic developments at some given period in time require that it shall function. If any society is to function well, however, Fromm says, its members must come to want to do what it is necessary that they shall do.[5]

[1] See her excellent essay, "Culture Change and Character Structure," in Stein, Vidich, and White, eds., *Identity and Anxiety* (New York: The Free Press of Glencoe, 1960), pp. 88-98.

[2] See also his "The Problem of Ego Identity" in *Identity and Anxiety*, pp. 37-87.

[3] David Riesman, *The Lonely Crowd* (New Haven, Conn.: Yale University Press, 1950, hard-cover edition), p. 4.

[4] See *American Sociological Review*, IX (1944), p. 380; also in Clyde Kluckhohn and Henry Murray, eds., *Personality in Nature, Society and Culture* (New York: Alfred A. Knopf, 1959), p. 515.

[5] *Ibid.*, pp. 517-518.

This might make one think that Fromm would require the person to adjust himself to the society in which he happens to have been born, to acquire, as it were, the character that best adapts him to function in that society. But Fromm also notes that so long as "the interest of the individual and that of society are not *identical* [my italics], the aims of society have to be attained at a greater or a lesser expense of the freedom and spontaneity of the individual."[6]

The views that Riesman, Erikson, and Fromm have put forward neglect the individual's instinctual drives, however. In their evading Freud's fundamental thesis, these three writers have overemphasized the significances of environment and society. Nevertheless, all three recognize the difficulty that modern man faces in his task of adjustment to society. Fromm and Erikson fall back upon the ancient prescription of using child training and education as means of fostering identification between the individual and his society.

Clearly, in modern American society the interests of the individual are by no means identical with those of many factors that are of prime importance to the society. We have already pointed out many of the ways in which it is difficult for the person to establish the needed identification between himself and his social environment; and unless a valid rather than pseudo identification is established, it becomes difficult to establish a valid individuation.

The conflict between the individual and his society has contributed to the development of that aspect of the modern identity crisis involved in the difficulty that he has in achieving identification with his culture. This difficulty, of course, is clearest to the observer who has some training and who also has achieved a measure of individuation for himself. But the difficulty is felt more widely, as is shown by the number of patients who come to psychotherapy with identity problems.

Modern mass society offers the individual many pseudo-gratifications along with the realities of food, clothing, and shelter, but, for all its increasing sexual permissiveness, it often seems to fail to meet certain basic instinctual needs. As Ernst van den Haag points out, too many Americans crave diversion with an insatiable craving because they are cut off even from knowledge of what they actually do want.[7] These persons have been so thwarted that they no longer are aware of their thwarting. They may feel a pervasive anxiety, a

6 *Ibid.*, p. 518.

7 "Of Happiness and Despair We Have No Measure," in Bernard Rosenberg and David Manning White, eds., *Mass Culture* (New York: The Free Press of Glencoe, 1957), p. 504.

restless *malaise*, but they have lost even the desire to live in a meaningful way.[8]

In this situation, men tend to become aimless and undirected and gradually submerge their individuality in the social character of their society. In our mass culture, people are led and directed and often can no longer act as individuals. Such persons have experienced that depersonalization which is so strikingly a trait of modern mass culture. Appearances have become the goal; the façade counts, not what is behind it, yet not even the façade is respected for long.

Hannah Arendt has noted the conflict between durability and functionality, between that which endures of itself and for its own sake and that which meets some need. Culture itself is threatened, she says, ". . . when all worldly objects and things, produced by the present or past, are treated as mere functions for the life process of society, as though they are there only to fulfill some need, and for this functionalization it is almost irrelevant whether the needs in question are of a high or a low order."[9]

If we consider only the "practical" aspects of the functions of society and the individual, we stand in danger of ignoring the intangibles, which are often more important than the functions themselves. But what happens when this relationship between the material and the spiritual has broken down and the transformation of one into another is ignored?

These aspects of what some call the crisis of mass culture bring us nearer understanding of the problems associated with culture identity. In a comparatively short time, external factors have brought about sweeping changes in the way people live and hence in their situation in society. Since 1930, the Western world has experienced the Great Depression and a Second World War; the United States has lived through the New Deal and a period of great technological development as well. It enjoys a great degree of prosperity, in spite of recurring soft spots in the economy, yet often seems unable to finance solutions for some of its recurring problems.

Of these, education may have received most attention, perhaps because of the pressure of international rivalries. Actually, American education has long been troubled by the need to deal with large numbers of people of exceedingly diverse backgrounds and levels of ability. From its beginning, the United States has had more people able to read, say, than was the rule in England at least. Later, when this level of

---

8 *Ibid.*, p. 534.
9 *Between Past and Future* (New York: Viking Press, 1961), pp. 197, 208.

literacy was threatened, notably by the movement of population into unsettled areas and by the immigration of illiterate peasants, Americans developed a commitment to education for everyone. Only through education could a population of most diverse origin become part of a common culture.

Consequently, the American school has long been an instrument of acculturation, deliberately used as such, as well as a place for intellectual and vocational training. And it may be said that the system has been successful in achieving its goal, for during the period between 1890 and 1920, millions of immigrants, mostly of peasant origin, have become part of the middle-class American world, accepting most middle-class values, including that of education as the ladder of social mobility.

Even later, when the United States closed its doors against peasant immigration from Southern Europe and when child labor was decreasingly profitable or acceptable, the American school, especially the secondary school, showed its capacity for becoming an important custodial institution. The school system faces new problems, however, for industry requires a declining proportion of the labor force and those it does need must have a higher level of education. Nor can the public secondary school effectively serve as custodian of those young people who drop out of school because they no longer see education as even nominally a ladder to higher levels of the social system.

Currently, American education faces two problems: fitting individuals to live in a technological mass society without losing too many of the traditional human values and, secondly, using the schools to bring the young people among the new immigrants to the big cities into the orbit of the middle-class world. The school system has been all but unprepared for this task, largely because it is in the hands of professional educators, administrators whose orientation is either toward business and practical politics—a necessity if adequate appropriations are to be secured—or toward the curious blend of watered-down psychology and diluted subject matter that is the staple of too many education courses. Educational policy is made by administrators and trustees; rarely is it made by scholars. For scholars are not genuinely respected in American society: even the scientist is regarded as a mere technician; only the man who has met a payroll is worth listening to on matters of social policy. Furthermore, the American *polity*, to use an old-fashioned word for the society seen as a political entity, is committed to dealing with problems as they arise. In fact, this usually means problems are dealt with piecemeal and often in ways that increase the impact of the total problem. Thus, the level of academic instruction has risen in secondary schools, but schools are not improving in urban slum areas, which often seem to be increasing as people are shifted in projects for urban renewal.

A second and even more vivid example of the piecemeal approach to problems is the issue of Suburbia. Americans always have cherished the notion of home ownership, even if that ownership represented a one-sixth interest in property held on thirty-year mortgage. Federal government support has made it possible for many people to secure mortgage credit and so achieve home ownership. To this aid, the current phase of Suburbia owes its being. The outward aspect of Suburbia is the work of builders, often operating for speculative profit rather than long-term investment. Sociological and psychological studies seem to indicate that the inward being of Suburbia is not in accord with its frequently pleasant, secure outward aspect. The emotional problems that beset those in the suburbs are far beyond normal proportions, as appears in John R. Seeley's study, *Crestwood Heights.* Seeley, like others who have explored, and in their exploring perhaps created Suburbia, does not deal with an identifiable individual community but rather abstracts from sociologists' observation of a group of communities, Canadian in this instance. Such studies, supplemented by inference from a great variety of material ranging between the comments of architects and the sometimes acrimonious discussions carried on in the correspondence columns of college alumni magazines, indicate that suburban life is hard on its beneficiaries. Men's irritations are obvious: money and time wasted in traveling. Women, especially educated women, often report frustrations with a pattern of life that limits their daytime associates to their children, female neighbors whom they have not chosen, and, occasionally, the deliveryman—although women are generally assigned the task of picking up the groceries, taking clothes to and from the dry cleaners, along with chauffeuring their children and husbands. The monotony of life in the suburbs has begun to provoke a small beginning of return to the cities, where the assumed needs of children do not interfere. For lonely as city life can be, its dismal vistas offer the privacy of anonymity at least. A woman may not know her neighbor in an apartment house, but she isn't likely to come in, coffee pot in hand, disrupting a morning's plans in the name of sociability.

The relation between Suburbia and the absorption of individuals by organizational commitments has not been explored to any great depth. Suburbia is usually occupied by organization men; but since most people are employed by some large organization or other, this is not a determinative element in the situation. Nevertheless the publicity of life in a suburb is not too unlike the regimentation of life in a large organization. And it is not without significance that some of the largest corporations are moving their offices out of cities to suburban areas. Such moves serve many purposes, but the concentration of employees in smaller communities does tend to deprive workers of the kind of protective coloration provided by residence in a large city. Leisure is supposed to supply some of the satisfaction that work no longer gives, but leisure may well become a continuation of work when it is spent in proximity to fellow employees who do not even have traditional class antagonisms to shield them as a group from the scrutiny of personnel staffs and other administrators who live nearby or are members of the same PTA. An active imagination might see the migration of white-collar enterprises to the suburbs as leading to a kind of private-enterprise Big Brotherism.

As has been pointed out, in a comparatively short time, external factors have brought about sweeping changes in the way many Americans live and hence in their situation in society. Cultural identity helps to denote the extent to which, at any given time, the individual can identify himself, in the broadest sense, with his social environment. Cultural identity is not limited to a few important aspects of life, such as one's family or occupation, but includes the whole cultural setting in which the personality functions. The cultural-societal identity is not permanent, however, since it is merely the sum of the individual identifications of the people in that society. In other words, it is a variable component in the permanent complex of society. Cultural identity, then, changes much more rapidly than social character, and there is room for both concepts in analyzing a society. The concept of cultural identity may be said to envisage society as if it were a never-ending motion picture, shifting from scene to scene and embracing all the aspects of individual crisis within it.[10]

Comparing identity and character in American mass society makes it possible to discover the phases of change that enter into crisis. It hardly needs to be repeated that contemporary American character today is predominantly other-directed; that is to say, for the past thirty or forty years, large numbers of persons have not only relied on the judgment of their peers in forming their tastes and opinions, but they have accepted

10 For man-in-transition *is* both his cultural identity and his cultural situation. In discussing contemporary American society, one may well speak in terms of man-in-crisis, people-in-crisis, and society-in-crisis.

this reliance as right and proper. Even fairly conservative nineteenth-century novelists—Thackeray, for instance—laughed at those who lived with an eye to what their neighbors thought and did. Now, living by such guidance is acceptable; even nonconformity has become patterned, as it were. Hipster and square alike, each looks to his fellow and few look within themselves. As Riesman remarks—putting what people have long known perhaps into peculiarly clear and striking phrases—men today have become exceedingly aware of the signals that indicate the view of others; they have, as it were, developed an inner mechanism that receives such signals and subsequently evokes from the personality those responses which are felt to be the desired ones.

Thus, Riesman sees the modern American operating by an internal radar, which is exquisitely sensitive to the "pips" which indicate that somebody is not approving. For Fromm, on the other hand, the modern American (who is nearest the type of "modern Western man") is an instrument of the capitalistic economy. And the American vernacular seems to bear out Fromm's contention that modern man is a marketer. For every university school of business and every do-it-yourself book on how to be a better businessman would make the first commandment in a decalogue of business success: you shall sell yourself with all your heart and with all your soul. Both the Riesman and the Fromm interpretations show man directed by the society in which he lives, but Riesman does not see modern man as alienated to the degree that Fromm does. According to Riesman, the satisfaction modern man has lost as a maker of things he can gain as a consumer of them.

Specific aspects of cultural identity are sometimes the same as specific aspects of the social character, such as those just discussed. The concept of cultural identity, however, reflects man and society in transition and makes possible the analysis of phenomena which are constantly changing. Cultural identity itself is a concept of change, a fact that can hardly be over-emphasized. So far as the specific characteristics of cultural identity in contemporary America are concerned, there is a dichotomy; that is, the characteristics that mark the life of man-in-crisis might well be shown as having both positive and negative aspects. For the moment, however, it does not seem feasible to explore these characteristic problems in a valuative way.

An outstanding characteristic of our time is the stress on adjustment as the proper goal toward which all men should strive in every aspect of their lives. Thus, people are expected to adjust to the prevailing standards and mores of their schools, their businesses, the social and other organizations they belong to, and their environment generally. Even in the work of historians, who once, in the name of science, refrained from judging the past, we see a tendency to extol conservatives and to scold reformers as ill-mannered, uninformed, and overemotional to the point of being proper subjects for psychotherapy. Currently, the burden of proof continues to be put on the person who points out a social abuse; he is all but required to produce evidence of mental health. And since acceptance of the social pattern appears to be one of the prevailing criteria of mental health, the reformer's path, always difficult, is now made difficult in a novel way: being "maladjusted" has replaced being "immoral" or "irreligious" as the appropriate stick with which to beat the person who causes discomfort.

Adjustment as a norm has further consequences, since it implies that people must adjust to themselves. For surely the unceasing stress upon adjustment implies an inner conflict for the individual, which has been cheerfully ignored by those who urge adaptation to the demands of the group as a good in itself. So far as the individual is concerned, efforts to make the adjustment required by the social group, and often all but enforced by educational and counseling institutions, have on occasion been detrimental to the individual's peace and happiness. So far as society is concerned, its current common aims may well be less worthy than those of the "maladjusted" individual. Acquiescence in the aims and practices of society, or rather of the ruling group in the society, contributes to the conformity and standardization that troubles many observers of modern American society and affect many persons who, perhaps, may not appear much disturbed or distressed by the demands of living in the contemporary industrialized world.

Many social scientists have discussed the impact upon American cultural identity of what they see as the increasing standardization of life.[11] A society economically committed to mass production of consumer durables needs must accept a large measure of standardization in the external aspects of its life. Inevitably, the question rises: can the person maintain his individuality in a standardized world, or will external standardization inevitably encroach upon the possibility of

11 For a wealth of material on this subject, see Bernard Rosenberg and David Manning White, eds., *Mass Culture* (New York: Free Press of Glencoe, 1957), and Eric Larrabee and Rolf Meyerson, eds., *Mass Leisure* (New York: Free Press of Glencoe, 1958). Also pertinent is a special issue of *Daedalus* (Spring, 1960) which was devoted to the problems of mass culture. The essays are reprinted in *Culture for the Millions*, ed. Norman Jacobs (Princeton, N.J.: D. Van Nostrand Co., Inc., 1961).

maintaining human uniqueness in any effectively meaningful way?

Again, in an economic world dedicated to the kind of production that requires mass consumption, it is not surprising that the culture be largely one in which the person secures his lines of direction from sources external to himself. Contemporary American cultural identity includes the idea that the individual cannot function without the aid and guidance of some group, an idea which may seem incongruous in a society constantly proclaiming its "allegiance" to the ideal of primary value of the individual human being. One need only read William H. Whyte's *The Organization Man*[12] to be aware of the extent to which organizations and, in particular, large-scale business organizations, have affected not only the conduct of public and private life, but even the individual's own view of life as such.

Finally, there is the affluence of American society, which has radically affected the lives of many individuals.

It will, I think, be agreed that these are all negative and perhaps undesirable aspects of our cultural identity. The inclusion of affluence in this list may seem surprising, but in many respects increased wealth has had a definitely detrimental effect both on society and on the individual. Of course, it is highly desirable that people should have goods that once they were unable to enjoy. Sometimes, of course, one wonders whether the new buyer gets what he wants, rather than what manufacturers and the advertisers who serve them want to sell. The wealth of society has sometimes had a disruptive effect on the integrity of the individual, a disruption that can be described in terms of the desire to get something for nothing. In an economy that rewards speculation rather highly, however, the line between acceptable and nonacceptable versions of getting something for very little (if not nothing) is rather hard to draw.

The increase in "white-collar" crime may be a more significant symptom. Again, offenses of this sort have been committed before. Their current prevalence and their alleged increase point up the difficulty that the individual in a mobile and money-oriented society encounters when he is tempted to break the rules in order to enjoy the goods that the mores tell him he needs, not only for themselves but also for their contribution to the welfare of his ego. Having goods, or the money that will buy them, makes many persons feel themselves more present, more truly existent, in the philosophic sense. Hence, an increasing number of individuals in the

12 (New York: Doubleday Anchor Books, 1957).

respectable middle class, which is most in accord with the current cultural identity, may well be committing crimes as a means of confirming themselves in their identity.

Another negative aspect of the growth of wealth in our society is the encouragement it seems to offer to the cult of "privatism," to the widespread feeling that the only place in which men and women can "be themselves" and feel the potential of achievement in themselves is in a private, family life, which seems increasingly to be more and more like the private and individual life of their neighbors. Concern with public problems is not fashionable. Only cranks, it is said, are troubled by depleted water resources and landscapes made ugly by haphazard real estate "development." Even though an increasing number of wealthy men hold political office, public life and public issues have lost prestige. Those who consider themselves well informed and animated by good will tend to concentrate on personal resolution of personal problems; they often avoid coming to grips with the need to achieve social resolution of social problems.

Consider some expressions of desire to do good to others. Certain charities that raise money for the support of refugees in Europe, the Far East, and even the reservations where American Indians live, publish the names and photographs of their more appealing charges when asking for contributions. The donor is promised *personal* gratitude. The beneficiary will write him and regard him as a foster parent. Thus the executives of charitable organizations use the misery of the people they are seeking to help in order to provide emotional satisfaction for contributors. This is not a new phenomenon, it must be admitted. Charity balls, with their attendant social publicity for the organizers and guests, have been part of the social calendar since early in the nineteenth century at least. In the United States, these events and the closely related "benefit performances" of plays, ballets, operas, and the like, have long been a path on which the possessors of new wealth achieved status in their communities. Engaging in good works, indeed, stands among the acceptable methods of social climbing, for it casts the mantle of charity over ostentatious spending and self-advertising.

The desire to receive recognition for one's good deeds is human enough, but exploitation of that desire as a means of selling patent medicines and other merchandise shows a curious lack of sensitivity both in the exploiters of people's woes and in those who seem to enjoy having their misery exploited. When radio was in its heyday in the 1930's, commercial sponsors supported programs in which individuals presented their most intimate woes to a counselor whose principal qualification for that office was a heartily unctuous voice in which he repeated clichés with the air of having made original moral discoveries. When it was revealed that one of these "counselors" advised a hair tonic enthusiastically although he was bald, and that another, who specialized in keeping marriages together, had been divorced eight times— audiences seemed to grow even more enthusiastic.

More recently, as the public has become somewhat better informed about psychological counseling, both radio and television programs have turned to procuring direct aid. Some of these programs seek to raise money for the direct relief of individuals and read the names of contributors for all to hear. In such TV programs as *Queen for a Day*, the recipient of the sponsors' gifts has to offer her misfortunes for the entertainment of countless viewers. Americans do give most generously to charities, but one wonders, however unworthy the doubt may appear, how much private giving is inspired solely by the desire to help the unfortunate. The activity of the professional charity fund raiser shows how thoroughly institutionalized even benevolence has become.

Interestingly, willingness to make gifts (large-scale philanthropy is sometimes called the "conscience money" of the American plutocrat, and the charitable or educational foundation the modern equivalent of the expiatory church or convent) is paralleled by reluctance to adopt the kind of social legislation common in most Western countries. Unemployment insurance, old age pensions, and prepaid medical care have long been the rule in industrialized Europe. To the European observer, it often seems odd that in the United States, which so extols individual independence, resort to the almsgiver in emergencies should seem so much more worthy of an upstanding citizen than his having a claim upon public provision for needs that he cannot meet out of his savings—the more particularly when a credit-based consumer economy operates to discourage saving, especially among the lower-income groups.

Thus far, stress has gone to the negative aspects of American cultural identity, to some of the flaws in the "American character" as such. Many of these flaws can be traced back to some of the difficulties that people in America have in establishing their identity both on the side of identification and on the side of individuation. Yet the picture of American cultural identity is not wholly depressing. Rebelliousness, especially among the young, is beginning not only to appear but also to be somewhat valued in certain key areas of the society. Some students in colleges and universities are showing greater interest in public affairs.[13] Some even indicate a willingness to become involved in political organizations or politically oriented groups. (Interestingly, the one set of organizations not highly valued in American society is that concerned with its government, that is, political parties and their factions.) The most conspicuous of the student activists are, of course, the Negro college students who have often risked their bodies in the effort to win recognition of their rights and the rights of their Negro fellow citizens. Many of these students come from small Southern colleges, often associated with evangelical denominations. In our time, much has been said about Christianity's lagging social influence at the very time when Christian churches were increasing their membership, when undergraduate programs were offering "majors" in religion, and when the study of theology was experiencing a revival in the intellectually superior areas of the Protestant communions; Catholicism had already imported its Thomist revival. The action of the Southern Negro students may be reviving a supposedly outmoded "social gospel" in unexpected form.

But rebelliousness on the campus is not limited to a revived political interest oriented toward repudiation of the lapses of the older generation, whether those lapses were from conservative principles or from failure to accept the challenge of society to deal with the unsolved problems arising from the changes occurring so rapidly. We see rebelliousness among young people in suburbs where some adolescents, at least, are showing dissatisfaction with the patterns to which they are required to adjust.

Perhaps the most vivid and disturbing phase of rebelliousness is what is called "juvenile deliquency." The young have always been refractory in the United States. Juvenile gangs and youthful ruffians are not new in American cities. New, however, are the scale of juvenile misbehavior and the lust for violence which that misbehavior often shows. Disturbingly often, youthful violence seems purposeless, motivated by desire neither for money nor for revenge, a true *acte gratuit* as that is described by André Gide. This characteristic striking out for its own sake seems to mark current juvenile delinquency as a blind attack upon a world that offers to non-white youth, at least, few genuine opportunities to share in the glories of the affluent society of the new "people's

[13] For an interesting discussion on this subject, see *The Nation*, May 27, 1961. All this issue is devoted to "Rebels with a Hundred Causes" and deals with the awakening of contemporary college youth to current problems. See also David Riesman's article, "Where is the College Generation Headed?" *The Atlantic*, April, 1961.

capitalism." But delinquency and purposeless violence are not limited to the poor of our great cities. Delinquents are found in the prosperous suburbs, too, although their acts may less often lead to punishment and publicity. There seems to be a growing "underground" current of resentment against the adult world. Such a writer as Norman Mailer can find a positive aspect to juvenile delinquency; these young people at least show desire for adventure, for a kind of personal fulfillment, which is denied them by a society that gives little room for the adolescent to grow as a person rather than as a member of an acceptable group. One must note, however, that the delinquent no less than the respectable seeks the psychological support of a group.[14]

A new emphasis on goals that run somewhat counter to prevailing norms points toward changes in American cultural identity. Thus, many persons are putting new emphasis on enjoying the arts and literature. Others are beginning to place a novel stress on privacy. This is encouraging because privacy is cherished by those who are aware of themselves as individuals; hence, although change comes slowly, even a slight reaction is to be appreciated. So we may think that a desire for the privacy of anonymity lies behind the return to the city that some observers see occurring. Nevertheless, life in the public eye is still an American rule. Suburban gardens have low hedges. Students in colleges not situated in large cities are often required to live in dormitories. Instructors are expected to leave their office doors open. Americans find it difficult either to withdraw from society for a time or to be alone within it. Even business, with the growth of conferences and "brainstorming," indicates its distrust of the man alone reaching his decisions and doing his work in privacy.

Most important, perhaps, is the emergence of nonmaterialist goals. To be sure, many persons who have a desire for such goals or who at least find materialistic striving unsatisfying, do not know what goals they may be seeking. Yet the search itself may be a truly positive goal.

We have seen that the individual develops his identity, or fails to do so, through identification and through individuation. Identifications bring a person into contact with the social character and the cultural identity of his time. Although cultural identity and social character are often confused, they are actually widely different. This chapter has given con-

14 Norman Mailer, "She Thought the Russians Was Coming" (*Dissent*, Summer, 1961, VIII, no. 3, p. 408). The negative aspects of the delinquent's rebellion may be found in Harry Slochower, "The Juvenile Delinquent and the Mythic Hero" (*Dissent*, Summer, 1961, VIII, no. 3, p. 413).

siderable attention to certain negative aspects of American cultural identity. Those aspects will be discussed in further detail in the following chapter, particularly as they tend to produce *anomie* in the social structure.

VI. CLASS AND IDENTITY

At this point, it seems appropriate to ask whether there are any links between social class and susceptibility to identity crises. The general social crisis in the United States is associated both with the spread and the breakdown of traditional middle-class values. As a society, the United States has long been both simply structured and mobile. The United States has had no feudal experience, unless we are to take the pre-Civil War plantation owners as the equivalent of feudal barons. And careful study of prewar Southern society shows that it was affected by social movement to a remarkable degree. Except for Negroes and Latin Americans of partly Negro origin, few Americans have been irretrievably marked as belonging to a particular class. In the United States, class lines are drawn rather largely by income and the living habits and education that income makes possible.

As many studies of the Warner school have shown, most Americans think of themselves as belonging to the middle class. It is that class which sets the social tone. And every white person at least aspires to become a member of the middle class. Currently, much of the emotional thrust behind the Negroes' demand for equal rights is supplied by resentment against being prevented from climbing the social ladder toward middle-class status.

Becoming a member of the middle class requires the acceptance of its ethos, its style of life, and, as we shall point out in a moment, that style of life makes for anxiety and a considerable measure of emotional instability. This is not to claim emotional stability and freedom from emotional disorders for members of the lower classes. Leonard Reissman points out that the middle-class susceptibility to neurotic conflict may help its members avoid psychotic disorder.[1] Hollingsworth's New Haven study notes the difference in diagnosis and treatment received by disturbed members of different social classes (that is, income groups). Since members of the lower classes are much less likely to receive psychotherapy than members of the middle class, their identity

[1] *Class in American Society* (New York: The Free Press of Glencoe, 1959), p. 268.

problems are rather more difficult to explore and understand. Furthermore, social pressure for acceptance of middle-class standards tends to assimilate lower-class identity problems with those of the group above. Indeed, in our current state of ignorance about the lower-class American (who does not study himself, as a rule, and is usually studied by the middle-class American only when he is in trouble) we might even say that identity problems in the lower class (when they are not really ethnic problems) may be interpreted as growing out of the effort of the lower-class person to establish a middle-class identification.

In a mobile society like ours, incidentally, the lower-class person may have fewer difficulties in identifying himself with middle-class mores than would a person of similar background in a less mobile society. This case of movement, in its turn, is not unrelated to the instability of certain aspects of the middle-class ethos itself. A trivial but perhaps significant instance may be drawn from the recipes in the higher-priced women's magazines. These journals have long been models of at least the lower middle-class notion of gracious living. Thirty-odd years ago, the food editors of these magazines instructed their readers to prepare good, wholesome, salt-and-pepper-seasoned Anglo-Saxon dishes. Now, peasant dishes of many lands are presented in all their herbal variety. The lower-class immigrant, risen to middle-class income levels, has imposed some of his own standards on what once might have been called "his betters." Thus we might say that the quality of shallowness in the middle-class ethos has contributed to its powers of assimilation.

The middle class is generally urban or suburban in residence, since its occupations are tied to the making of money. In a highly developed modern economy, fewer and fewer individuals make (or grow) things, and more and more of them "shuffle paper" as the invidious phrase would put it. Currently, about 8 per cent of the American people live on farms and a proportionately small number serve them immediately. To a much larger degree than is true of less mobile societies, contemporary rural America (again exclusively the South and Southwest with its Negro and Mexican native-born aliens) shares the technological benefits and the socio-economic problems of contemporary mass society. Rural people have aspirations that are as middle class as those of the blue-collar worker; more so, perhaps, since the American farmer has traditionally made money (when he did make it) as a land speculator, since he is frequently an employer, and since, when he is successful, he produces for a market and not for his own use. There may be an American rural personality, but this apparently shows itself in a fondness for peculiarly raucous music and a devotion to political clichés rather than in notably stable identity structures. One might perhaps see in the continued movement from farm to city not only a response to lack of economic opportunity, but also an inability to achieve identification with the rural way of life.

The identity crisis is most visible in urban and suburban areas, nevertheless, and its consequences are most evident in the middle-class family. The contemporary middle class, as John R. Seeley notes, is identified with the role of management[2] and particularly with what the textbooks in business administration call *middle management*. This group transmits decisions from the top, or decision-making level, to the bottom or production level and reports results from the bottom level to the top. Middle management is intensely competitive, for it wants to rise to the decision-making level. It is intensely prudent, for exercise of judgment may alienate someone just above who has power to evaluate performance. It is occupied primarily with manipulating people; middle management "gets things done" through influencing people, not through mastery of engineering or other physical techniques.[3] (And middle management stands in the shadow of obsolescence for a principal current objective of the computer technician is the development of programs that will reduce or, hopefully, eliminate middle management as it reduces personnel.)

Middle-class life is concerned with *action, organization,* and *control.* Spontaneity would be destructive to its aspirations. Contemplation might cause wonder about the validity of what a man was doing or how he was living. And, like Tennyson's Light Brigadier, his is "not to reason why." His goals are prescribed. His means for reaching those goals are also prescribed; generally, they are dictated by the organization that pays his wages and, in many instances, determines which "American way of life" he shall actually lead.

A man who examines either goal or method for achieving it enters upon a perilous enterprise. For if goal and method should be critically examined, the examiner might find them empty. And such an emptiness would confront many persons with the unbearable, the meaning or nonmeaning of existence itself. If neither goal nor method is examined, worse, if individuals are obscurely aware that neither can bear examination, then identity problems are likely to surface, as it were. From the depths, the individual is prodded by the recurrent questions: Who am I? Where do I belong? Do I belong?

2 John R. Seeley *et al., Crestwood Heights* (New York: Basic Books, 1956), pp. 356-357.
3 *Ibid.,* p. 359.

Education and economic opportunity make it more likely that the middle-class person will verbalize such questions; other persons may be troubled without knowing how to put their trouble into words. It is also likely that those in certain age groups are going to be peculiarly affected by identity problems. Will it be the middle-aged who have internalized the societal changes of our time? Will it be those in the thirties who have an established way of life but still may "kick against the pricks"? Or will it be the adolescents who, as Erik Erikson has observed, are involved in an identity crisis by the very fact of being an adolescent?

One may ask whether the crisis which is adolescence affects the formation and growth of total personality more than it did in earlier times. American teenagers may be more turbulent than their grandparents, but we should remember how many of their grandparents were playing adult economic roles at least: in the 1890's, most sixteen-year-olds were earning their livings at manual labor of one sort or another and many middle-class youths were at work in offices. The notion of the teenager as someone who is necessarily at school and only partly, if at all, self-supporting dates to the Depression (only in 1940 did the United States Census stop counting the labor force as all those over ten years old). If we may take novels as evidence, the adolescent and his problems were usually treated as a joke until well after the First World War. The general attitude toward adolescence has indeed changed in our time; growing up is no longer considered to be a matter of adding years and assuming economic responsibilities; rather it is a "problem." Again, this is particularly true of middle-class America where the adolescent must often make his own decisions and carry on a continuous dialogue with himself and others in order to find out what is best for him in any particular situation.

The teenager is offered guidance, to be sure, but that guidance may come from parents and other adults who often behave more like competitors than like guides—as might be expected in a society where youth is so much a cult that even parents are reluctant "to act their age," in the slang phrase. With the current pattern of youthful marriage, parents frequently can appear to be their children's chronological contemporaries and frequently seek to do so. For years, however, parents have been acting less as parents and more as the peers of their own children; as he struggles to become an adult, they involve him in their own lack of identity.

Within the range of my observation as sociologist and psychotherapist, the lack of identity is most felt by young parents—persons between their late twenties and early forties.

The peculiarly ambivalent involvement of such persons with their children's problems, and the increasing complexity of those problems, especially among adolescents, seem related to the failure of such parents to provide an adequate parental image. Some of these parents appear to regard themselves as "afflicted" with the parental role (a not unreasonable attitude when one considers the American's desire to remain too young to be the parent of anyone older than an infant). Yet when these youthful parents belong to the middle class, which is proverbially oriented toward duty, they cannot leave their adolescent children to cope with their personal problems as best they may. Such parents seek advice, and counseling agencies multiply to meet the demand. With the supply of counsel thus available, it becomes almost obligatory to employ it; often one is provoked to think that providing psychotherapy for one's adolescent children confers status, perhaps higher status than skiing lessons or orthodontic treatment.

More seriously, the resort to professional counsel indicates parental unwillingness or inability to help solve their children's problems because they cannot cope with their own. Yet recognition of the need for counseling is more useful than is dismissing adolescent crises with old-fashioned catch phrases: "Johnny is going through a difficult period" or "Janie will settle down in a year or two."

The contemporary teenager appears peculiarly unable to communicate with his parents. Social scientists have not paid too much attention to what may be seen as a new kind of alienation between child and parent, but that alienation exists and can be understood in terms of the identity crises being experienced by many parents. The factor of role-confusion has already been mentioned. Our mobile society has blurred many patterns of expectation: girls should be able to count on learning the feminine role from their mothers, for example, but often their mothers do not know how to play that role. It is difficult to learn how to become a woman in a society which honors youth alone. Nor, in such a society, is it any easier to learn how to be a man. The boy, like the girl, is apt to find that his father has not truly learned the man's role. And boy and girl alike find it difficult to identify parents as parents. Instead, children often find it necessary to encounter their parents as peers and competitors. The teenager's relationship with such parents becomes confused and distorted and may lead to serious psychological disturbances. The disturbed relationship has contributed to the disappearance of effective parenthood, which is one of the most essential elements in the functioning of society. This situation may very well account for the failure of educators to cope with the problems of adolescents. The normal identity crisis of adolescence is complicated and intensified by the teenager's unsatisfactory relationship with parents who tend to repudiate the parental role, partly because the depletion of their own identity has led to the absence of valid life-goals.

The heart of the identity crisis is thus in the family—the family whose life and standards are rapidly changing today. This is as true of affluent suburban families as it is of poverty-stricken and underprivileged metropolitan families. The energetic adolescent has become a rebel: "a rebel without a cause." The adolescent has no real cause for rebellion against middle-class parents who think that the best way to deal with teenagers is to leave them alone. Still less need such an adolescent rebel against parents who want nothing better than that he be "well adjusted," that is, acceptable to his peers and not too obviously troublesome to his teachers. Such parents may well be totally at a loss when such adolescent children become delinquent: vandals without apparent anger, car thieves without apparent need, assaultive toward strangers, sexually promiscuous. The middle-class parent pays for the damage caused by his sons when necessary and conceals the pregnancies of his daughters, should they occur. The lower-class parent must leave his children to the law. Parents of both groups tend to be equally bewildered, however. And the professional employees of legal and social agencies are no less bewildered by the delinquent behavior that does not seem to stem from deprivation. The delinquency that comes from the deprivation of the modern slum is itself of a new kind, but this problem is more appropriately dealt with in another chapter (Chap. VII).

Parents themselves, often without knowing it, are caught in identity crises. They experience one aspect of those crises as persons who will not accept (perhaps because contemporary society makes it so difficult for them to find) the appropriate parental role. It is difficult for them to discover what that role should be in the contemporary world. Nor are these parents of ever-larger families secure in their social position. They often feel trapped in a society that makes increasing demands upon them. They often feel without an aim, even one related to their position in the family. Parents in this position feel frustration but rarely do they express this in rebellion, even in the kind of rebellion represented by an effort to look at themselves, their goals, and their world with critical understanding.

Thus the relations between parents and children are deeply involved in the identity crisis, which so often occurs within the *family-in-crisis*. Not that this excludes the individual for, as already stated, the crisis of the individual in the mass society is intense and evident. Yet in investigating the specific aspects of the individual's situation, it becomes increasingly obvious that, in *this* society, many crises of identity take place within the context of the family which has, as it were, slipped its traditional moorings and developed few serviceable new ones.

Many individuals, of course, encounter their identity crises outside the family. They are lonely, as we shall see. Often they can no longer identify with their traditional occupational and professional roles. Artisan and craftsman have already lived through this experience. The farmer's traditional role has also begun to elude him. The middle class has found it more possible to identify itself with its economic role than have other economic groups, but that identification has become more difficult for even the middle-class person to find in contemporary society. Perhaps it is for this reason that middle-class Americans are so concerned with interpersonal conflict. A large number of them, in the current retreat from politics, have ceased to be interested in social and political methods for dealing with group tensions. Conflict between individuals seems particularly disturbing. Yet, paradoxically, it often seems that only in conflict can a person in the alienated middle class experience "the other" as an existential reality.

Recently, sociologists, journalists, novelists, playwrights, all have been occupied with problems of human relations in the upper and middle levels of American society. Such concern is not new, of course, but there is a new, deeper sense that men, and especially middle-class men, are shut within walls of separateness. The emphasis points to a kind of breakdown, which extends far beyond the middle class proper. The functioning of the structure of the middle class, with its emphasis on competitive achievement—almost from the cradle to the grave—and on the manipulation of persons as the means to achievement tends to produce anxious, other-directed individuals. But, as has been pointed out, the United States is so mobile a society and the middle class so universally its model that middle-class values and problems become the problems and values of the society as a whole.

Middle-class values do not exist alone, however. Nor are they the only factor operating to produce the current crisis of identity in the United States. Such historians as Carl N. Degler would deny that "other-direction" was new in the United States or that identity problems are completely novel. Culturally, the American has always played "follow-the-leader."[4] The mass media have constituted a highly developed business, at least since Frank Leslie first published his illustrated weekly or the *Police Gazette* provided lightly clothed buxom beauty to titillate the male eye while he waited for his weekly shave. Conformity has been exacted from Americans since the legislators of the seventeenth-century colonies tried to tell women how much property their husbands must have before their wives might wear silk hoods and lace collars. Society offered fewer choices of role before the twentieth century, however; hence identification was easier. Rapidly as social values changed, the pace was less swift than it has become. For most of the truly uprooted, the peasant immigrants who became the machine fodder of mine, mill, and factory, the movement was from the one social depth to another, identity might be troubled but it was not lost. In our century, the identity crisis has sharpened because values themselves have altered. Their alteration has been sharpest in the middle class, some of whose values persist even to obsolescence, whereas others have been transformed or distorted. Amidst this social confusion, psychological confusion grows and the identity crisis has intensified until it seems almost to constitute a way of life.

VII. ANOMIE AND IDENTITY

Before exploring the relationship of *anomie* and identity, it is necessary to examine certain aspects of the concept of anomie itself. Emile Durkheim, who established *anomie*, literally meaning "normlessness," in the vocabulary of sociology, tied the concept to the emergence of industrial society. In his study on suicide,[1] for example, he noted that national suicide rates generally increased with a rise in national prosperity; suicide rates were lowest in the poorest countries. Durkheim interpreted this as indicating that industrialization was prone to weaken the sanctions of culture; as industrialization and the consequent prosperity increased, anomie or normlessness would appear; the country concerned would experience societal disorganization either in the form of the breakdown of organizations and societal groups, or in the disintegration of the individual in society.

Since the study of anomie is still in its early stages in America, we have no integrated and complete study of anomie

[4] Unpublished paper by Carl N. Degler.
[1] *Suicide* (New York: The Free Press of Glencoe, 1951).

in the United States. Among the few significant American contributions to the contemporary theory of anomie is Robert K.
Merton's essay "Social Structure and Anomie."[2] We do, however, have a few studies that use the concept in dealing with
such instances of social disorganization as juvenile delinquency.[3]

The concept of anomie is extremely helpful in analyzing the
current identity crisis, for that crisis both brings anomic
aspects of our society into prominence and is affected by
those social stresses. In this chapter, I shall discuss the disintegration and disorganization of societal and individual
identity in terms of the specifically anomic behavior evident
in our society and try to understand such behavior in terms
of the identity crisis. Phenomena such as juvenile delinquency,
mental illness, and sexual deviance are, in our society, anomic;
they are also closely related to the question of identity.

A number of factors contribute to the disintegration of both
personality and society in modern America. Among the most
important of these factors is role confusion and role expectation, that is, the prevalent uncertainty about the demands of
each of the many different places in the structure of society
that a person may be called upon to fill.

As I have said earlier, a dynamic society such as ours requires the individual to make many more choices than a
static society would offer. A man can choose whom he will
marry, and where he will live, and how he will earn his
living (in theory, most careers are open to talent and, even
in practice, the individual has a wide choice of different kinds
of work). In less dynamic societies, all these decisions may be
made for him. If the person must make these choices for himself, his life necessarily becomes more complex. The freedom
of choice, which is an outstanding characteristic of a secular
society such as ours, is the hope of democracy; but it is also a
basic cause of social disorganization. Ability to choose of
itself imposes a certain degree of instability. In our society,
moreover, freedom of choice is actually rather limited. Stress
on freedom thus becomes even more conducive to social
disorganization. Energetic individuals who have absorbed real
belief in the attainability of the theoretically available goals
often attempt to reach them in ways less approved socially

2 *Social Theory and Social Structure* (New York: The Free Press of
Glencoe, 1957). This chapter is reprinted in *Varieties of Modern Social
Theory,* Hendrik M. Ruitenbeek, ed. (New York: E. P. Dutton & Co.,
Inc., 1963).

3 Richard A. Cloward and Lloyd E. Olin, *Delinquency and Opportunity: A Theory of Delinquent Gangs* (New York: The Free Press
of Glencoe, 1960). The authors analyze the structure of a juvenile
gang, based on Robert K. Merton's *Social Theory and Social Structure.*

than the kind of competition for money and status that is considered the true end of man in our society. We may take the number of persons who try to reach their goals by socially forbidden methods as a clue to social disorganization.[4] In the essay to which I have referred Merton lists five methods of adapting to the demand of society in achieving the goals it prescribes, namely, conformity, innovation, ritualism, retreatism, and rebellion. The social structure of the United States, Merton observes, tends to produce anomie and deviant behavior because it stresses success, and competition in order to achieve success. The emphasis on success has percolated into every social stratum and every area of human endeavor. At the same time, there has been a weakening of social and psychological controls over what means may be used for achieving success. More and more persons seem to have absorbed the social philosophy of classical "economic man" in which "calculation of personal advantage and fear of punishment are the only regulating agencies."[5]

Modern industrialization requires the general use of goods that might have been considered luxuries in an earlier day. In the United States, the economy is very largely based upon the need to market such consumer durables as automobiles, refrigerators, TV sets, and all the gadgetry that characterizes modern life. We are said to live in a consumption-oriented economy, but we might more accurately be said to consume in order that others may produce so that they, in their turn, may be able to consume.

Such an economy depends on the operation of a huge anonymous market. Such an economy permits and, increasingly, even requires a high level of mobility: persons change their occupation, residence, and associations with unprecedented frequency. The application of technology to agriculture has made it possible for a smaller (and shrinking) proportion of the population to produce food for a whole society, although both the total population and per capita consumption of food have increased. Consequently, the country has seen a great shift from the country to the city, or at least to metropolitan areas. Even persons who live in the country are urbanized; they see the same TV programs, they read the same features and same comics in their newspapers; they buy the same clothes at shopping centers of the kind that good roads and the ownership of automobiles make as accessible to rural people as to those who live in the suburbs.

4 Mabel A. Elliott and Francis E. Merrill, *Social Disorganization* (New York: Harper & Brothers, 1961), p. 26.
5 Robert K. Merton, "Social Structure and Anomie" in *Social Theory and Social Structure* (New York: The Free Press of Glencoe, 1957).

Industrialization and mobility, as Ernst van den Haag puts it, "increase the frequency of contacts with strangers and decrease the continuity of all contacts. There are more people and fewer persons in most lives."[6]

In the phrase, "more people and fewer persons," we may sum up the disintegration of personality produced by the anomic pattern of our society. It is also quite literally true, for modern urban man, moving from place to place and from job to job, encounters a large number of people for short periods of time. His situation may be contrasted with that of a villager in a less dynamic society who knows a few persons intimately for a lifetime. One need not labor the significance of this state of affairs in terms of identity; when the human environment is reduced to a series of fleeting contacts with strangers or near strangers, man can no longer find security in the continuity of his environment. In this situation, identity is endangered, for it is bound to reflect the discontinuity of the social environment: a man living in so mobile a world will be less sure of himself and of others than a person in more stable surroundings. The more persons a modern man "knows," the fewer he relates to in genuine ways; often, he feels he can put lasting trust only in his immediate family circle—and family ties themselves lack stability.

The development of the "scientific mentality" has also had a disruptive effect on the social structure. New developments in technology have directly helped to uproot tradition and the social structure. At the same time, scientific advances have helped develop a general expectation of constant change. The good old days and the good old ways are constantly praised. Sometimes "back to McKinley" seems to be the most effective political battle cry. Nevertheless, social groups constantly shift and change, their norms decay or are confused. Obviously, the dilution of the authority of norms in our society has contributed to the disintegration of individual identity. It is very difficult for the individual to preserve his identity in a society where traditional social groups and institutions no longer offer firm support. If, for example, a man finds that the family no longer is the most important social group in determining his role in society, but has been replaced by economic organizations or by peer groups, his confusion will be increased.

In a highly organized society such as our own, the importance of group organization has risen and an increasing number of persons can become part of such groups. Yet, in

6 Ernst van den Haag and Ralph Ross, *The Fabric of Society* (New York: Harcourt, Brace and World, 1957), p. 105.

so mobile a society, group membership is often short-lived. Group as well as individual relationships tend to become more shallow, less differentiated, more interchangeable, as it were. In large companies, particularly, as Whyte points out, "people can move all over the world and never meet anybody but other company people—and be quite happy that they don't."[7]

If friends are easily replaceable, relationships have taken on a new color, a kind of characteristic impermanence. And when relationships are so impermanent, those who engage in them are increasingly apt to experience a fragmentation of their identity. Under the circumstances of modern life, only a person with deeply rooted values and a firm sense of his individuality can maintain the sense of identity that makes life in a mass society endurable. Yet that society, as too many persons experience it, fails to give the person the body of identification and the support out of which he can build the ability to differentiate himself as a unique person, aware of his uniqueness and drawing strength from it as he draws strength from the bonds he feels with his fellows.

In modern America those bonds seem increasingly slack; a kind of shallowness has come to characterize the relationship of individuals. They seem almost afraid of intimacy because it makes them feel their dependency on those around them; a deep and permanent relationship seems overly demanding, a threat to identity. Yet individuals, often the same individuals, have withdrawn from involvement with the public world and retreated into personal relationships. Many observers of American society see the development of life in Suburbia as an expression of this "privatism," this investment of life and emotion in the family. Yet, as has been mentioned, the family is a fragile institution, as the divorce rate indicates, and life in Suburbia is often devoid of privacy: its lawns are unhedged; its back doors stand ajar; its neighbors are, perforce, friends.

Women, and perhaps the suburban housewife in particular, suffer in peculiar ways from the lack of support that their society gives them in establishing their identity; their problems both reflect the larger societal situation and radiate out into that situation. The plight of the suburban housewife was fairly realistically portrayed on an NBC TV program[8] but, although a sociologist and a psychologist supervised the presentation, the suggested solution seemed something less

7 William H. Whyte, Jr., "Individualism in Suburbia," *Confluence*, Vol. 3, no. 3, September, 1954.

8 NBC TV program, "The Trapped Housewife," broadcast on July 25, 1961; also published in: George Lefferts' *Special for Women*, introduction by Margaret Mead (New York: Avon Books, 1962).

than plausible. The harried housewife need only say a re-
sounding NO, and she could stop taking tranquilizers. The
problems of individuals trapped in the identity crisis of our
time are not thus easily resolved.

One aspect of that crisis may be seen in the curious simul-
taneous movement away from intimacy and deep relationships—which are felt as threats to identity—and toward
immersion in groups. Americans want to *belong,* yet there
seems little worth belonging to. For social and religious bonds
have been extended, blurred, disassociated from each other,
and often weakened. Economic bonds have been strengthened,
however; in many instances, "the company" has fallen heir to
loyalties that once belonged to friends, family, church, or the
state itself. "What is good for General Motors is good for the
country" might be spoken by many persons besides the man
who was charged with having said it, and might apply to a
broad range of social interests. Meanwhile, the individual is
entangled in so many ties to so many organizations that he
feels more like an interchangeable part and less like a person.
This is the situation that leads to a search for identity for,
entrapped in the web of organization, man feels "strange,"
isolated, and alienated. Confronted by freedom of a kind
never known before, the person feels stripped of protection,
fearful of being swept into "the vastness swirling about us."[9]
And in the very organizational shelter that the individual
seeks and finds, he feels swallowed up and alien, the more
isolated, the more he is surrounded.

And surrounded he is, for privacy is becoming more and
more of an unknown quantity in American life. The absence
of devices permitting temporary retreat from society is in itself
a sign of the completeness of the conquest of privacy: Americans live behind open doors in offices and dormitories, as has
been mentioned. They are not allowed to keep their names
to themselves: the receptionist and the bank teller sits behind
a little notice announcing his name to the world; even the
waitress wears her name embroidered on her bosom. Fake
personalization, in the sociologist's phrase, has replaced real
regard for persons. Retirement into solitude has ceased to be
an opportunity offered by daily life. Where [besides the bath-
room] can a man go to be by himself?

The very desire may seem suspect. The person is forbidden
to go away because he is the property of his environment and
his group and has an obligation toward them. This resentment
of any display of desire for a truly separate existence is not
unrelated to the perverted concept of loyalty that is peculiar

9 Ernst van den Haag, *op. cit.,* p. 106.

to America, among the free societies of the world. The loyalty to the environment demanded of the individual in America goes far beyond the normal needs of society, in a way that is both astounding and shocking. Loyalty is no longer merely a question of political loyalty to one's country. "Un-American" can now be applied to anything from lack of interest in baseball to a desire to bring the welfare state to this hemisphere.[10] "Keeping his nose clean" has become many a citizen's chief objective; he seeks to avoid contamination from persons and ideas that may be considered "controversial," which has become one of the dirtiest of dirty words (although it is neither four-letter nor Anglo-Saxon). In this kind of social environment, personal integrity is threatened on many levels; indeed one may question whether integrity is not obsolescent in the world one can see emerging.

Industrialization, urbanization, the growth of wealth, the decay of tradition, the retreat from public concern and deeply held personal relationships, all the characteristics of a society that says it is based on individualism and thwarts the expression of individuality contribute to the disintegration that is anomie. Identity problems and anomie are closely related, as will become clearer when we consider juvenile delinquency, sexual deviance, mental illness, and the confusion of moral standards, of ideas of right and wrong.

The causes of juvenile delinquency are numerous, though scarcely as numerous as the social scientists who have written on the subject. Yet the plethora of books, papers, and reports on the subject justifies the current view that many of the conditions commonly considered as the main causes of juvenile delinquency are actually no more than contributory factors. Slum housing, for example, long considered a prime cause of delinquency and crime, is today recognized as merely a symptom of the defects in the structure of our society that may be responsible both for poverty and for the difficulty that many young people find in becoming part of our middle-class world.[11] Poverty itself cannot be considered the basic cause of contemporary juvenile delinquency, for the phenomenon is evident in Western Europe as well as in the United States and Western Europe has rarely been so prosperous. German sociologists even talk of *Wohlfahrtskriminalität*, the criminality of prosperity. Erik H. Erikson discusses the hardness and defiance shown by juvenile delinquents, and

---

[10] Those interested in the political aspects of loyalty should not fail to read the illuminating report on the HUAC in Frank J. Donner's *The Un-Americans* (New York: Ballantine Books, 1961).

[11] Ernst van den Haag, "Notes on New York Housing," *Dissent*, Summer, 1961.

interprets it as the reaction to the application of complicated and outdated laws that have little relevance to the behavior of the delinquent young.[12]

In reality, however, juvenile delinquency is primarily a problem of the individual, the problem of establishing an identity. The central problems of juvenile delinquency are questions for the psychoanalyst, not for the sociologist. Psychoanalysis sees the precarious position of the adolescent, struggling with suddenly and greatly intensified sexual and aggressive drives; it focuses on the individual's inner need for an identity and a consistent morality. The sociologist can most effectively contribute to dealing with juvenile delinquency by studying how society can offer the young person a variety of roles in one or more of which he can establish his identity. For, as Erikson observes, society offers occupational and status roles—each with its recognized appropriate manners and rewards—for the young person to "try on," as it were. Since choice is all-important in this area, the sociologist studying juvenile delinquency must be particularly concerned with the number and adequacy of the roles society presents for the adolescent to choose from. It is important to realize that once a young person has chosen a role, even though the role is that of a delinquent, he is committed to it, for in assuming that role he has acquired an identity, however unsatisfactory it may be and however desirable it may seem that such an identity should be temporary.

Harry Slochower and Norman Mailer both note that often the juvenile delinquent is groping after the kind of heroic ideal that society either does not supply or supplies only in thin and shoddy form. In American cities, particularly, the delinquent finds neither relevant norms nor useful support in the dominant middle-class society. To Mailer, the members of delinquent gangs may have more of the stuff of life in them than their bloodless middle-class elders.[13] Slum adolescents are the delinquents that trouble society—the car thieves whose parents can't pay for the damage they cause, the sex offenders whose parents can't afford abortions or military schools, the vandals who have no one to pay the bills, the assailants whose victims bleed and die publicly and without compensation. These adolescents attract the sociologists' and the social

[12] Erik H. Erikson and Kai T. Erikson, "The Confirmation of the Delinquent," *Chicago Review*, Vol. 10, no. 4, Winter, 1957; also in *Psychoanalysis and Social Science*, Hendrik M. Ruitenbeek, ed. (New York: Dutton Everyman Paperback, 1962). See also, "The Teddy Boy International," *Encounter*, August, 1961.

[13] Norman Mailer, "She Thought the Russians Was Coming," *Dissent*, Summer, 1961.

workers' attention along with that of the police and the courts. Yet few of those concerned with delinquency are aware of its broader implications. They become so involved with the details of incidental palliatives, such as neighborhood projects, that they cannot themselves recognize the identity crisis of the young, much less confront adolescents with it.

No longer can individuals achieve the relatively easy identification that could be achieved, that was actually enforced, in earlier phases of Western history. In rhetoric, at least, the easy, enforced identification has been replaced by individual freedom. But freedom imposes a burden of choice. Men must learn, individually, by their crime and suffering, to know themselves. It seems almost an existential tragedy, and is certainly one of the paradoxes of the "affluent society," that our young people cannot make more fruitful use of the freedom that they have gained more recently than their elders. For long after even the poor had acquired the vote and the right to organize and strike, young people were still subject to a very broad range of parental authority. Increasingly, and particularly in the United States, young men and women have tended to escape parental control, the more particularly when they are able to earn their own living. Yet their failure cannot be attributed entirely to their own deficiencies. Because of the lack of communal identification, young people must learn what society expects of them through a trial-and-error process. This is particularly true of those who come from "marginal" homes where parents are poor and so far outside middle-class culture that its norms are not norms for them, but ill-understood and resented compulsions.

Society itself, including educational institutions, is experiencing the anomie, the normless quality, described at the beginning of this chapter. Such a society can scarcely make adequate efforts to cope with juvenile delinquency. Paul Goodman touches the nub of the problem in *Growing Up Absurd* where he notes that our society offers young people neither work nor challenge; the best opportunity it gives is the opportunity to become corrupt. In a society that "has no Honour . . . has no Community," it is small wonder that young people struggle with identity problems. Their relationship with society has broken down and is unlikely to be restored by palliative juvenile delinquency programs. Psychologists and social workers directly concerned with delinquents are diverted from underlying issues by the sheer bulk of immediate problems. Efforts to deal with the drug addict, the thief, the "mugger," the young prostitute, the fourteen-year-old unmarried mother, leave small room for deep and far-ranging social inquiry. Efforts to cope with the emotional disturbances of the middle-class adolescent give little greater encouragement to real appreciation of society's contribution to the identity crisis as it affects young people.

The obvious young delinquent and the disturbed middle-class adolescent in treatment (or in trouble that often goes unpublicized) both show evidence of being affected by an identity problem and that problem is very much a part of the identity crisis of our society today. The lower-class delinquent, particularly, exemplifies the entire situation. He is the product of societal anomie. He is the result of the appalling contrasts between the technological advances and the wealth displayed in our large cities and the restriction of opportunity to share in that wealth that affects the increasing nonwhite population of those cities. The delinquent is the result of an educational system completely unable to fulfill his needs, although it is hard to envision any educational system capable of meeting the needs of young people who feel excluded from opportunity. It might be said, incidentally, that the educational system is inadequate to educate in the old meaning of the word, however well it may be suited to induct the majority of the young into the rituals of a competitive, mass society dedicated to consuming in order that others may produce.

Above all, the juvenile delinquent is the result of the general insecurity, anxiety, and loneliness that adults experience. Somewhere between childhood and adulthood the delinquent becomes fixed in an identity crisis that he tries to solve with the only means at hand: crime and especially crimes of violence or, alternatively, relief from pressure through the use of narcotics.

Increasingly, psychologists and sociologists are concerned with the problem of sexual identity in America. Since deviant sexual behavior is closely associated with the breakdown in identity that constitutes the current identity crisis, the problem is appropriately discussed in this chapter.

The character of American society has been greatly influenced in matters of sexual identity by two largely unrelated phenomena: feminism and Freudian psychology (and especially psychoanalysis). Even married women enjoy the status of adults; they may own property, and make contracts independently of their husbands; women vote; and women earn their own livings, sometimes in high-status occupations. The emancipation that began in the nineteenth century and has accelerated since World War I has changed women's position in society and in the family. The family itself has changed in consequence, and with that change has come confusion. As

Kardiner points out, hard-and-fast sex role differentiations have tended to fade.[14]

Thus the child is increasingly apt to experience problems arising from the confusion of role identity. The family—that is, the parents—still provide the scene where roles develop and patterns of behavior are formed. If roles are blurred and patterns unclear, the child tends to grow up in the midst of psychological confusions, which generate problems of identification. Currently, Mother often works outside the home, as Father does (perhaps earning as much as Father does), participates in formally organized social activities outside the home, as Father does, and owns property—perhaps more than Father does since it is often advantageous for a man to put property "into his wife's name." Mother wears trousers, sometimes; she drives a car; she plays strenuous outdoor games; on occasions, she drinks, and gambles as well. The outward marks of sex role differentiation are unreliable. Here again, modern life offers a decreasing degree of merely external support to the establishment of identity. The conditions of modern life, and particularly the need of many middle-class women to work in order to maintain the standard of living, often tend to induce identity crises in women who must be sexually glamorous, economically competent, and psychologically skillful; mistress, mother, housewife, breadwinner: all of them at once. Small wonder that many women do not know what to expect of themselves or resent what they think is expected of them. Small wonder, too, that husband and children also are confused.

As the role of women has become blurred, the role of men has also changed. The powerful paterfamilias has had to become an equal partner, sharing authority not only with the wife but also, in America at least, with the children. Secondly, even male sexual dominance has been encroached upon by the current revival of emphasis on women's "rights" in this sphere. Certainly one of the impacts of psychoanalysis upon the popular culture has been a stress upon the role of sexual satisfaction in the normal and fruitful life. One might even say that American susceptibility to the Puritan ideal of duty has meshed with psychoanalytic insights and produced widespread conviction that inadequacy in the sexual sphere is equivalent to inability to secure promotion and salary raises.

In response to the incompletely assimilated changes in the economic and psychological circumstances of family life, the relationship between the sexes shows imbalance, not only

[14] Abram Kardiner, "Social and Cultural Implications of Psychoanalysis," *Psychoanalysis, Scientific Method, and Philosophy* (New York: New York University Press, 1959), p. 100.

within the family, but in society in general. This imbalance has been responsible for rising levels of adultery, divorce, promiscuity, and homosexuality. It may seem strange to classify such "normal" behavior as adultery and divorce as sexually deviant behavior, but since divorce, particularly, equally with homosexuality, expresses the breakdown in traditional relationships between men and women, the sociological significance of high divorce rates marks the growth of anomie in our society to almost as great a degree as homosexuality itself.

The causes of homosexuality, of course, go far beyond the recent breakdown in family life (as is obvious from the fact that homosexuality occurs in even the most stable societies). Freudian psychoanalysis explains the phenomenon in terms of the Oedipus complex, but we must recognize that homosexuality has no one readily identifiable cause or group of causes. Abram Kardiner, for example, believes that the apparent increase in homosexuality is traceable to an increase in the general difficulty of adaptation and to confusing or inconsistent cultural directives and restrictions. In other words, it has become harder for the child to place itself as boy or girl in the context of his family; further, he often is unable to internalize the image of right and wrong, normal or abnormal, because his parents themselves are not sufficiently certain of cultural directives to be able to impose useful bounds upon the activities of their children. As is common knowledge, many parents cannot cope with their children's emotional problems, and this inability—itself a breakdown in their *parental* identity—may help to cause a breakdown in the sexual identity of their children.

Kardiner points out the relationship between a competitive society's demand for economic success and sexual performance on the one hand and the development of male homosexuality on the other. Men, Kardiner says, are ground "between the compulsory public ideal of achievement of the higher living standard and the dread of a collapsed self-esteem."[15] Often, they feel exploited by women, a feeling to which the educational system—largely in the hands of women—contributes, as does the frequent absence of the father from daily life. For in spite of the shorter working week and the ideal of "togetherness," suburban life means a father present principally on week ends when his behavior often seems to represent not strength and ultimate familial authority, but rather indulgence and refuge from the discipline

15 *Ibid.*, pp. 101-102.

and demands, the authority, which mother and teacher represent, particularly for the preadolescent.

In her relationship with the father in the family, the mother tends to be either restrictive or demanding, pressing, albeit tactfully, for greater economic effort as provider or, on the contrary, exerting influence to restrain economic adventurism: investments, or purchases she sees as unwise. In the mother's relationship to the boy, she often seems castrating: whether she prods for "manly" activity, such as athletics, or whether she tries to protect her sons from the dangers of existence, the middle-class mother, at least, represents all the influences that seek to check male assertiveness.

The society itself, meanwhile, exerts certain relatively emasculating pressures. Passivity, compliance, and manipulation are traditionally regarded as female characteristics in Western society. As has been pointed out by students of the economic scene particularly, with the declining role of direct production and the increasing importance of marketing activities, ability to do, to control things, has become less important as a way of achieving success than ability to manipulate persons.[16]

What Kardiner describes as the flight into homosexuality, like the flight into promiscuity, or even the flight into marriage, thus is rooted in the character of a society which makes maximal demands on the individual and gives him minimal support in the process of developing and maintaining identity. "The upkeep on masculine ideals has gotten too high," Kardiner declares. Some young men seek security in early marriage and immersion in the gracious family living so glossily portrayed in the "home and family" magazines. That security seems somewhat less than rocklike, however, when one considers the pattern of divorce rates for young marriages. Other young men have given up efforts to establish genuine relationships with women and have taken the lurid sexual path.

The incidence of homosexuality is hard to measure, of course. Some writers think it is the awareness rather than the practice of homosexuality that has grown. Certainly, the degree of general public familiarity with homosexuality is astounding, compared with the situation in continental Europe. The current popularity of *City of Night* is an instance in point. Certainly its place on bestseller lists shows how markedly American attitudes have changed. Twenty years ago, a novel about the world of the homosexual prostitute would have been

[16] Wright Mills, *White Collar* (New York: Oxford University Press, 1956).

prosecuted under some obscenity statute—unless, perhaps, it were shielded by the prestige of a great and foreign name. So far as is known John Rechy marks no eminent literary figure; nor does the novel have any high degree of literary merit. But 40,000 or more persons have shown their interest in homosexual experience by spending the $5.95 needed to buy the book.

To my mind, this increase in awareness is evidence of an increase in homosexual practice. Nevertheless, we still have no really reliable data on the number of confirmed homosexuals in the United States; estimates range from Kinsey's 6 per cent to Jess Stearn's 16 per cent.[17] Indeed, any serious sociological study of homosexuality in the United States is hard to find; the few articles that have appeared in professional journals are inadequate from the sociological point of view. Some autobiographical material is available but that must be discounted for personal bias; journalistic reports such as Stearn's tend to be superficial.[18] The problem of homosexuality requires exploration in the context of the disintegration of norms.

To the development of this context, the concept of identity makes a valuable contribution. Today, we see a general identity crisis in which a problem of sexual identity plays a significant part. Homosexuality is not only a symptom of the problem of sexual identity as part of the general identity crisis affecting the society. Like divorce, juvenile delinquency, and mental illness, homosexuality also reflects personal disorganization and interacts with the anomie which characterizes our time.

The problem of many American homosexuals is primarily one of identity. Whatever the valid psychoanalytic explanations for any particular case of homosexuality, the homosexual in America has to establish a sense of identity in a society that is not only hostile, but itself in crisis. The environment generally offers neither understanding nor support. This situation probably accounts for many homosexuals seeking psychological sustenance within a closed group, which often behaves like an organized minority of the more familiar ethnic sort.

Deviant sexual behavior whether in terms of promiscuity, which is often associated with the identity crisis of adoles-

17 Jess Stearn, *The Sixth Man* (New York: Doubleday & Co., 1961). R. E. L. Masters, *The Homosexual Revolution* (New York: Julian Press, 1962), is still more superficial.

18 The serious reader can find useful material in my anthology: *The Problem of Homosexuality in Modern Society* (New York: E. P. Dutton, 1963).

cence—much fostered by the fading of positive goals and parental authority—or of homosexuality will probably increase. For pressures on the family continue to promote its disintegration and the society will have to face the increasingly anomic consequences of family disintegration.

When we turn from juvenile delinquency and homosexuality to mental illness, we pass from identity confused to identity lost; for many varieties of mental illness, and particularly schizophrenia, represent an acute degree of failure to meet a personal identity crisis. One of the most striking anomic aspects of our society is the social problem of mental illness. Certain sociologists, among them Robert K. Merton, maintain that there is no evidence that the incidence of mental illness is any greater today than it was a hundred years ago. This, like the question of the incidence of homosexuality, is largely a matter of interpretation. Valid statistical comparison with the situation a hundred years ago is impossible because we do not have adequate data for the earlier period. In any case, whether there has been an actual rise in the number of cases of mental illness is largely an irrelevant question, since it is the degree of public awareness of mental illness that is useful in assessing its existence as a social problem. It is the place of the mental patient in the societal picture that is important in the present discussion. As with homosexuality, awareness has increased; this in itself indicates that mental illness is a much more serious problem in our society than it was a century ago. Certainly, no one can deny that modern man faces much heavier stresses and strains than his predecessors. The comparatively static society of the past has been replaced by one rapidly changing in every direction. In this society, as has been pointed out, it is difficult to establish identity. The person who completely fails to establish his identity, whether because of faults in his own psyche or because of lack of cultural direction from society, is placed under grave strain and may well become schizophrenic.

Schizophrenia offers the individual an escape from a reality that is more than he can endure; hence, in the situation of strain that reality imposes, it is not surprising that there should be a real increase in the incidence of schizophrenia. Kardiner attributes the increase to the structure of our society. Arthur Burton goes further, declaring that the schizophrenic's encounter with such phenomena as the Absurd and Nothingness (which may be expressed in loneliness, aloneness, isolation, and estrangement) points to general defects in our whole culture as such. Nothingness, in the existential sense, is the absence of full identification. This feeling manifests itself in dread, anxiety, and flight;[19] and one can see evidences of both the feeling and its manifestations in what we call *normal* life. Burton goes so far as to say that the reality of our time is of such a kind as to evoke a general schizoid retreat.[20] And Burton seems fairly accurate when one considers such phenomena as the intellectual's retreat from the public world, whether one turns to the contemporary play, novel, picture, poem; one sees creative people turning inward, away from an unbearable actuality to fantasy spun from within and then projected as cares about which the less creative can weave fantasies of interpretation.

The retreat characteristic of the schizophrenic patient is an important way of escape for the person whose identity no longer makes sense to himself or, for that matter, to his family and friends. Retreat may be the *only* escape for the person who is beset by anxiety and who has fallen into total despair; he feels trapped in the complexities of our society and takes the only way out he can find. The schizophrenic has failed to maintain and sometimes even to establish the identity that linked him to the world. He is no longer, in Heidegger's terminology, a being-in-the-world, and strenuously resists any attempt to bring him back from the world of the Absurd because his absurdity has by this time become predictable and reliable for him. He has found a false identity.

In such cases, the psychiatrist must attempt to restore the patient's identity, which is often completely "lost." But the psychiatrist's task is often impossibly difficult. For the schizophrenic has lost both awareness and responsibility. He "experiences" himself as so limited in his full humanity that he can no longer feel himself as really "existent." These are the qualities of the schizophrenic experience that made Kronfield call schizophrenia "anticipated death."[21]

The relationship among anomie, identity, and schizophrenia in our society is thus clearly evident. The extreme consequences of anomie may bring a man into a situation where he cannot realize the norms and values of his environment; his identity is in danger of disintegrating. Under such stress, the ultimate escape is flight from reality, flight from the complexities, choices, and responsibilities of mass society, from large-scale organization, from obligation to groups, from the web of suburban living. With its escape from choice, schizophrenia (and in a sense all mental illness) is a condition

19 Arthur Burton, ed., *Psychotherapy of the Psychoses* (New York: Basic Books, 1961), p. 172.

20 *Ibid.*, p. 173.

21 V. Frankl, *The Doctor and the Soul* (New York: Alfred A. Knopf, 1955), p. 251.

in which man has no present, only a past. And however unhappy that past, it at least is not a set of contemporary demands.

Another type of mental patient, in some sense characteristic of our society, is the manic-depressive. As with the schizophrenic, here the mental patient is extremely significant for the sociologist concerned with problems of societal anomie and identity. Edith Weigert describes the manic-depressive as though he carried to a "logical" conclusion the imperatives of a society that encourages the person to depend on others for even his current directives rather than to incorporate into himself commands sufficiently stable to enable him to move toward goals of his own by making decisions he feels to be his own.[22]

To put it otherwise, Weigert thinks that both the manic-depressive patient and his world are *impoverished,* which is indeed true in a mass society such as ours, with declining and confusing standards of behavior.

Many persons in our society feel trapped, or even suffocated (a feeling that is responsible for the break-up of numerous marriages). Many feel that in some way they are not authentic, and daily ask themselves, and often others, "What makes *me* an individual?" These manic and depressive moods—for that is what they are—are signs of the generally anomic situation, and are a common experience for persons in our society. Of course, such moods were experiences in the past, too. Erik H. Erikson has, for example, identified and analyzed them in Martin Luther,[23] and in so doing has brought to light the serious identity crisis that Luther underwent. But today the incidence of manic-depressive moods is sufficiently frequent and widespread to constitute a societal symptom. For the contemporary patient to restore his identity calls for understanding and effort. The *credo quia absurdum,* Kierkegaard's "leap into faith," is an essential part of the process. It is equally essential that the therapist be aware of the social and cultural situation and the patient's setting in society, for it is here that the clue to the recovery of the lost identity is often found.

The foregoing discussion of juvenile delinquency, deviant sexual behavior, and mental illness is far from complete. This discussion has sought to link certain aspects of these phenomena to the presence of anomie and the problem of identity in our society. Each of the phenomena surveyed here is an

22 Edith Weigert, "The Psychotherapy of the Affective Psychoses," *Psychotherapy of the Psychoses,* Arthur Burton, ed. (New York: Basic Books, 1961), p. 351.
23 *Young Man Luther* (New York: W. W. Norton & Co., Inc., 1958).

outgrowth of our society's state of anomie; each is a manifestation of the current identity crisis. The following chapter will discuss the search for identity in mass society, with special emphasis on the problems of personality common to members of such a society and the strains to which that society subjects them.

VIII. IDENTITY IN AMERICA

This chapter discusses those aspects of the identity problem that are particularly useful in the general interpretation of contemporary American society. Although we have many valuable studies of the interaction of individuals in American society, analysis of the American image remains a pertinent field of inquiry. For with all the studies available, exploration is still necessary, since Americans and their society continue to change and to change in the direction of complexity. The rate of social mobility, moreover, makes it more and more difficult to make validly significant statements about the behavior patterns of individuals in contemporary American society. Current changes, furthermore, are going on so rapidly that they have tended to distort even the social scientist's perspective.

Despite these rapid changes and the confusion these changes have engendered, the student of American society sees some kinds of behavior that resemble those noted by de Tocqueville more than a century ago. This suggests that, even in a society as dynamic as ours, basic assumptions do continue to hold good for America and its people. Those basic assumptions form the American image, as it is seen both at home and abroad. Can this image be used as the setting for an interpretation of identity in America? I think it can.

In speaking of basic assumptions, I am not referring to those superficial characteristics that are often and erroneously made the decisive elements in interpreting American life. Americans are indeed generally friendly; they express themselves frankly and openly, are unperturbed by details, welcome progress and new developments, and are nearly always in a rush. But these traits do not provide any real clue to the American identity, to the true image of the American.

If we may speak of a national image, of national identity, and national identity crises—always aware that such generalization requires most delicate caution—what constitutes the image of the American? As important, perhaps, out of what experience does that image emerge? The European observer cannot but see that, in American society, crisis is the norm. From the beginning, persons and institutions in America always have existed in a situation where present states of flux have made previous states of flux seem periods of stability. One might say that the American identity and its crisis have developed from this at least statistical norm of change. One might go further, perhaps, and wonder how much and how rapid a change people can experience without threat to their sense of identity.

It has been argued that the pressures of modern mass society are responsible for the present crisis of identity in America. One may see that crisis as an existential tragedy. All existence has a tragic quality, for the conditions of man's existence in the world require men to choose and to act; and, on occasion, whatever their choice may be, the outcome of the action which that choice entails will not be good. In the contemporary world, many a person stands confronted with such situations. To refrain from choosing, to drift with the tide, is itself a choice. Many an American makes that choice, incidentally, and often he suffers, unaware of the reason for his suffering, even, at times, unaware that he does suffer. The middle-class American at least is surrounded with opportunities for happiness, yet he struggles to achieve a sense of belonging; he cannot solve—often he cannot even face—his innermost problems. The observer often feels that the American lives in disguise: he is caught in a web of social demand and unable to achieve full development of his individuality. Often, he feels obliged to conceal what is truly individual in himself. Such concealment ultimately brings a sense of unrelatedness to the external world; the person feels empty; he lacks direction, as the psychologist might say. Even if he has a chosen goal, it often seems to lack meaning. He pursues success, say, because the pursuit is expected, but he may no longer even enjoy pursuing, let alone finding the genuine satisfaction that he gets when the goal is reached.

Mass society and its contemporary demands are not sufficient to account for the crisis; one must look deeper. We have already noted the centrality of the child and childhood in American life. Nowhere in the Western world is there so much emphasis on the child. This is not new, of course; the American child has long held the center of the stage. He has long been called precocious, long asserted his right to a place in the grown-ups' world, to have an adult's privileges, to have some of an adult's responsibilities.

American society changes so rapidly, however, that even this pattern of child development has tended to disintegrate under the demands of an increasingly urbanized society, which has less and less need for the unskilled young person, which offers him fewer apprenticeship opportunities, fewer chances to learn a vocation merely by taking a place at the bottom of the ladder and which, at the same time, keeps thrusting before his eyes all the materially desirable goods that it tells him are the proper things to be desired.

In the eighteenth century, children were dressed as adults but they were expected to behave as children: to learn from adults and defer to them. Currently, it seems that American adults dress themselves as adolescents and apparently defer to their children. Where deference does not occur, as among recent immigrants of Latin origin particularly, the effort of parents to maintain Italian or Spanish cultural identity, say, often creates sharp conflict between the generations, with ambitious young people, particularly, repudiating their parents and becoming more American than the "Old Americans" themselves.

Among Americans of longer standing, the cult of youth, which has long affected American behavior, is curiously paralleled by pressure upon children to reach toward a pseudo adulthood. Everywhere except intellectually, the American child's development seems to be pushed; he lives in a kind of social hothouse. That a six-year-old should "be graduated" from kindergarten in an academic cap and gown may be absurd, but it is a symptomatic absurdity. That sixth-graders should have "proms" and 12-year-olds dates is even more symptomatic. Most revealing, however, are the many reports of parents organizing to resist adolescents' demands for unrestricted social privileges and to impose rules of behavior. One scarcely knows which is more "American," the need of parents to secure outside support in controlling their children or the issuing of what amount to public rules governing adolescents in their everyday social behavior.

One might accept pressures toward precocity if those pressures made for effective adaptation to adult life, but they do not—unless we take the "teenage" credit card as appropriate initiation into the realm of what Riesman calls "conscientious consumption." Adequate preparation for the adult role requires first that the child be encouraged to live a child's life, concentrating on physical activity and enjoyment and on academic preparation. Within this area, the child should be encouraged to take on an increasing measure of responsibility. In this way, as he grows, he is more adequately prepared for his adult roles than he is by engaging in precocious pseudo-adult activity. Currently, the demands of these activities—the requirement that even the ten- and twelve-year-old girl be "popular with boys," for example, tends to exhaust children before they become adolescent and to empty adolescents before they can become adults. Once again, we see the role of confusion that does much to deflect the development of a secure identification and thus to thwart the growth of real individuality: not the dog-eat-dog competitiveness, which often is called individualism, but the kind of confidence that allows a person to know himself and to be the self he knows, improving its behavior and increasing its accomplishments, perhaps, but secure in acceptance of his uniqueness.

Some Europeans regard the American personality as simple, but this cliché does not withstand examination. The American's easy accessibility, his openness, and his warmth often exist in a self-conscious person, one not merely concerned about how others regard him but about how he should regard himself. The American may talk brashly, but often that brashness hides self-distrust. Even the efficient American businessman, the hard-bitten maker of decisions may, in his business life, continuously try to shift responsibility to the person who is at the next level above him on the organization chart. For persons in less important positions economically, living has almost of necessity become a matter of dividing the personality, of being one man at work, another man at home, a third man in suburban public affairs, a fourth man at the country club. To live out so many and often such contradictory roles would be difficult even for someone who had a secure identity. For a person whose identity is not firmly established, role-playing can become even more confusing; the personality tends to become a many-layered covering for a hollow space within; one seeks a core and finds only emptiness.

Complexity and emptiness are both related to what van den Haag calls the "frightful" discontinuity of American life; they are also related to refusal to see the discontinuity for what it is and to assume that the "eternal verities" continue to be relevant in their old form although the context in which they must function grows more fluid year by year. In some respects, of course, American life does face up to American reality. So, we have "planned obsolescence" to provide a continuous market for consumers' durables. We are developing a "trade-in" market for houses so that people can change their homes, as they change their cars, to show their increased incomes. And, as has been mentioned, the mobility of the middle-management group has tended to increase very markedly. The cynical, noting the significance of very large enterprises in the economy, might see in these companies, with their national and international branches, a kind of privately operated garrison state whose personnel can be shifted about on order and must fit in wherever they may be dispatched. Increasingly, indeed, technical knowledge becomes less important to business success than does the ability to "fit in." Once again, maintaining identity is made difficult by the very external circumstances that require that a person have a stable identity if he is to remain in command of a genuine self.

In a changing world where tradition is at once desired and beside the point—like the "old world charm" of a roadside tea room or the "real home-made flavor" of canned noodle soup—large-scale intellectual activity seems increasingly difficult for the individual. The study of social problems is so divided and subdivided that it often seems unrelated to reality. Some of this division results from the aping of the respectable physical sciences by the aspiring social studies; some of it is the proper outcome of unwillingness to generalize until a sufficient body of relevant data has been accumulated. Yet, too often, data are expected to speak for themselves; a coherent picture of society is supposed to emerge from sketches with all too limited background in theory. Students of contemporary America, for example, fail to see how the separate problems that confront them are symptomatic of a larger problem, the present crisis of identity in the United States. We have numerous thought-provoking inquiries into such aspects of American society as mass culture, mass leisure, Freudian and neo-Freudian psychology, suburbs, the "trapped" housewife, the glamorous American secretary, and the plight of the American male. All these help us understand today's world, of course, but few sociologists have attempted to build an intellectual frame of reference into which these separate studies could be placed. And even fewer persons, among the ranks of professional social scientists or outside, seem to show energy and concern sufficient to use studies of problems for anything more than release from the stigma of ignorance and relief from the obligation to act.

Everywhere, in fact, from the psychoanalyst's couch to the articles "exposing" evils in newspapers and magazines, one sees the desire to "take it out" in talk. Contemporary social scientists are greatly concerned about the fate of man in mass society, but they often fail to see that it is not mass society in itself that is responsible for the sorry lot of the individual, but rather the inadequate preparation for his social role that this particular mass society gives the individual. Complaint about the increasing importance of organizations and the secondary role of the individual within such organizations does not solve the problem. The root of the matter lies with the individual, who is unable to withstand the pressure of the organizational trend and allows himself to be imprisoned within it.

Similarly, for two decades, social scientists have been concerned about some aspects of suburban life. John R. Seeley's *Crestwood Heights,* Maurice Stein's *The Eclipse of Community,* and a number of other studies all justify Riesman in talking about the "suburban sadness." The label is not unwarranted, as one can see from the rate of consumption of tranquilizers in these mortgage-loaded, picture-windowed dormitory facilities—communities they can scarcely be called because too many of them are mere halting places, designed for impermanence and lacking even the limited economic variety possible in the one-industry town. Nevertheless, we have small evidence that those who live in Suburbia are really concerned about what is happening to them. One does hear murmurs of discontent, of course, and psychotherapists do get numbers of patients from these areas, but one feels that these people are resigned: their lives have been laid out for them; they can neither change the pattern nor escape from it. Even to suggest the possibility of large-scale action to produce social change has become suspect. Conformity is a prime virtue. Even in revulsion against conformity, people tend to conform; they drop the pattern of Suburbia for the pattern of Bohemia, perhaps, the annual trade-in for the Volkswagen, the installment plan patio for the travel-now-pay-later trip to Europe, the Book-of-the-Month Club for the paperback. Even so much exercise of choice may show desire for a more self-determined way of life, but the movement often seems to be from one set of external imperatives to another.

Tocqueville showed his usual perceptiveness (or his distaste for what he saw as the wave of the future) when he declared that Americans were producing and would suffer from an organizational society. His observation forecast the later shift from inner- to other-direction. Perhaps the concerned sociologists are in error, therefore, perhaps the American is actually finding his real identity as an empty vessel waiting to be filled by the output of the assembly lines and the mass media.

Yet the psychoanalyst who sees evidence of disquieting personality trends, of alienation from themselves, from others, and from society and an even greater sense of loneliness in the midst of "togetherness" cannot believe that the American individual, beset by loneliness, despair, and alienation, ignorant of social challenge or of Utopian ideals, has finally found himself as he really is.

In most contemporary Western societies and in the Communist world as well, men seem in retreat from politics, as we have been told; they are no longer concerned with ideologies and ideals. The public world seems a hopeless place; only in private life can men seek valid satisfaction of their needs. Too often, however, the American, insofar as his identity is uncertain, can have no truly private world. Nor does retirement from political concern leave him with an entirely easy conscience.

So we see such phenomena as the growth of right-wing extremist groups and the mass media in quest of national purpose. In the 1920's, an oddly assorted group of prominent persons—millionaires, statesmen, popular writers, clergymen—might be asked for their opinions on Prohibition or the "flapper" (teenager to us); in the 1950's, similarly, miscellaneous assortments of individuals are asked for their opinions on national purpose. We go further, however, for the President appoints a commission to search for and state a definition of national purpose. No one asks why we need such a commission; still less does anyone wonder (out loud) whether such a commission can do anything useful. No one seems to realize that in the nature of things no mere inquiry or statement can provide a sense of purpose for the individual in society (and national purpose is after all the sum of many individual purposes). Such a purpose is either there or—unhappily—not there. The search for national purpose seems regrettably like the current educational emphasis on "direction," "self-expression," "creativity"; both the search for purpose and the stress on the creative seem to indicate the absence of ability to create or to move toward a self-selected goal.

It is easy enough to poke fun at a quest for national purpose, indeed, at all the "definition-making and purpose-guiding" organizations that clutter the American scene. Yet many persons take such activity seriously, and even more are willing to accept the slogans and formulas developed by such organizations. And often the slogans accepted come from ultraconservative groups. The urge to be active in the American Legion, the D.A.R., or the Christian Crusade Against Communism does not come from personal participation in World War I or II, from ancestral participation in the Revolutionary War, or even from desire to protect religion. Rather, such activity seems associated with an inability to achieve a genuine and deeply rooted sense of existence and identity. Because society is of such little help in giving individuals a sense of direction through identification with values usable in contemporary terms, right-wing groups seek values in a past "dimly seen through the mists of desire" (to paraphrase the *Star Spangled Banner*). In an often hysterical fashion, the "radical right" is thrashing about trying to find sound footing, although ideals are depleted and false values prevail.

Too many Americans are totally unaware of the true meaning that their traditional statements of national purpose, the preamble to the Constitution and the opening paragraphs of the Declaration of Independence, could have; for "Utopian" has become a dirty word; idealism a joke; consistency, ridiculous. Yet, "rallying around the flag" and calling oneself "a real American" is a poor substitute for public integrity. Sloganeering may simplify life, of course. It helps some men to assert belief in human equality while they deny Negroes the vote (and even, sometimes, the opportunity of hearing white ministers tell them how to get to heaven). It helps other men close their eyes to reality: to poverty and the denial of opportunity to many of their equal fellow citizens. It even allows men to talk about the human dignity of all individuals while forcing persons of low income to seek charity rather than providing prepaid medical care which is pretty much the rule in the rest of the civilized world.

The failure to cope with identity crises is thus evident in the society as well as individuals. On the one hand, the individual is all but submerged in organizations, economic, social, and academic. On the other hand, there is a widespread refusal to use political organizations for furthering the public welfare. Technical skill may evoke respect but, in politics, every man's ideas are considered as good as every other man's and the man who has no ideas at all is considered especially well suited to hold public office. The society as a whole, though it claims to be based on freedom, seems to fear the untrammeled interaction of political ideas.

As we have said, transition, not stability, is the American norm; crisis is our natural state of being; search for ideals, our ideal. Yet currently the search seems abandoned by too many persons; ability to live in crisis seems to make us confuse emptiness with comfort. Nevertheless, "Who am I?" and "Where am I going?" are questions heard all around.

Traditionally, the answer to the second question has been supplied by religion. And religion is experiencing a revival today. Yet religion, like other aspects of American life, seems enveloped in a perpetual *gloom* of optimism. Many Protestant sects, and even some Catholic parishes, are more inclined to concentrate on strawberry socials than to deal with "the dark night of the soul." Although American Protestantism nurtured the early sociologists in this country, there seems little sociological sensitivity, little passionate concern for the betterment of society in many American churches. We do have noteworthy exceptions, of course; Paul Tillich and Reinhold Niebuhr do challenge social complacency, many Northern white clergymen have joined the Negro's fight to be accepted as a first-class citizen and an equal member of the church. By and large, however, it seems that churchmen are inclined to believe this would be the best of conceivable social worlds if only more people preferred church attendance to golf.

No one can offer any pat prescription for dealing with the identity crisis. We may, however, hope for a gradual increase in general awareness of the nature and dimensions of the inseparable identity problems of society and of the individual. Obviously this calls for new approaches to education, to politics, and to the manifold problems of operating contemporary mass society by the rules of a free-enterprise economic philosophy that glorifies thrift, accumulation, and "the small producer." The person in search of identity must continue to live in a culture that provides no "pause for transition." Society will continue to be unstable and to afford the individual little external support. The economy will continue to be dynamic, based on the obsolescence not only of things but of people as automation transfers more and more tasks from man to machine. Social mobility will continue to be a demanding opportunity. The family will continue to be an uncertain refuge. The distrust of intellect will make many persons succumb to pseudo religiosity and to the pseudo politics of the radical right. The left will probably continue its attempt to keep its skirts unflecked by communism; the labor movement will continue to concentrate on "pork chops," to watch its membership fall off and its limited influence grow less. Psychoanalysis will offer some persons a refuge and even an opportunity to re-establish their identity. In general, however, maintaining and developing true identity will require that the person learn to distinguish the real from the illusory, the important from the trivial. He must come to realize that his stability depends on the extent to which he can find counsel in himself rather than in others. Man's identity is an essential part of his being: he can only assert it by refusing to take his societal environment entirely for granted and by continuous and critical self-questioning.

BIBLIOGRAPHY

ALBEE, EDWARD. *Three Plays.* New York: Coward-McCann, Inc., 1960.

ALEXANDER, FRANZ. *The Impact of Freudian Psychiatry.* Chicago: University of Chicago Press, 1961.

ARENDT, HANNAH. *The Human Condition.* New York: Doubleday Anchor, 1959.

———. *Between Past and Future.* New York: The Viking Press, 1961.

ARTZ, FREDERICK. *The Mind of the Middle Ages.* New York: Alfred A. Knopf, 1959.

BARZUN, JACQUES. *The House of Intellect.* New York: Harper and Row, 1959.

BELL, DANIEL. *The End of Ideology.* New York: The Free Press of Glencoe, 1960.

BETTELHEIM, BRUNO. *Love Is Not Enough.* New York: The Free Press of Glencoe, 1950.

———. *Truants from Life.* New York: The Free Press of Glencoe, 1955.

———. *The Informed Heart.* New York: The Free Press of Glencoe, 1960.

———. *Paul and Mary.* New York: Doubleday Anchor, 1961.

BOCHENSKI, I. M. *Contemporary European Philosophy.* Berkeley and Los Angeles: University of California Press, 1961.

BOWDEN, EDWIN T. *The Dungeon of the Heart.* New York: The Macmillan Co., 1961.

BRETON, GABRIEL. "Challenge—Who Needs It?" *New University Thought,* Summer 1961, Vol. I, no. 4, pp. 18-22.

BROWN, J. A. C. *Freud and the Post-Freudians.* Baltimore: Penguin Books, 1961.

BROWN, NORMAN O. *Life Against Death.* New York: Random House, 1960.

BRUCKBERGER, R. L. *Image of America.* New York: The Viking Press, 1959.

BUBER, MARTIN. *I and Thou.* New York: Charles Scribner's Sons, 1958.

BURCKHARDT, JACOB. *The Civilization of the Renaissance in Italy.* New York: Harper Torch Books, 1958.

BURTON, ARTHUR (ed.). *Psychotherapy of the Psychoses.* New York: Basic Books, 1961.

CAMUS, ALBERT. *The Stranger.* New York: Alfred A. Knopf, 1946.

———. *The Myth of Sisyphus.* New York: Alfred A. Knopf, 1955.

———. *The Rebel.* New York: Alfred A. Knopf, 1956.

CLOWARD, RICHARD A., and OLIN, LLOYD E. *Delinquency and Opportunity: A Theory of Delinquent Gangs.* New York: The Free Press of Glencoe, 1960.

COHEN, ALBERT K. *Delinquent Boys.* New York: The Free Press of Glencoe, 1955.

COHN, NORMAN. *The Pursuit of the Millennium.* New York: Harper Torch Books, 1961.

———. "The Cult of the Free Spirit: A Medieval Heresy Reconstructed," in *Psychoanalysis and the Psychoanalytic Review,* Spring 1961, Vol. 48, no. 1, p. 51.

COMMAGER, HENRY STEELE. *The American Mind*. New Haven: Yale University Press, 1950.

CORY, DONALD WEBSTER. *The Homosexual in America*. New York: Greenberg, 1951.

Dissent, Special Issue on New York, N.Y., Vol. III, Summer 1961, no. 3.

DOBRINER, WILLIAM (ed.). *Suburbia*. New York: G. P. Putnam's Sons, 1958.

DONNER, FRANK. *The Un-Americans*. New York: Ballantine Books, 1961.

DURKHEIM, EMILE, *Suicide*. New York: The Free Press of Glencoe, 1951.

———. *The Division of Labor in Society*. New York: The Free Press of Glencoe, 1960.

ELLIOTT, MABEL, and MERRILL, FRANCIS. *Social Disorganization*. New York: Harper and Row, 1961.

ERIKSON, ERIK H. *Childhood and Society*. New York: W. W. Norton and Co., 1950.

———. *Young Man Luther*. New York: W. W. Norton and Co., 1958.

———. "The Problem of Ego Identity," *Journal of the American Psychoanalytic Association*, Vol. IV, no. 1, 1956, pp. 58-121. Also in *Identity and Anxiety*, ed. Maurice Stein *et al*. New York: The Free Press of Glencoe, 1960, p. 37.

———. "On the Sense of Inner Identity," *Health and Human Relations*. New York: McGraw-Hill Book Co., 1953.

———. "Identity and Uprootedness," in *The Condition of Man in Modern Society*, ed. Hendrik M. Ruitenbeek. New York: G. P. Putnam's Sons, 1962.

———. "The Problem of Identity," *Journal of American Psychoanalysis*, Vol. IV, 1956, pp. 56-121.

ERIKSON, ERIK H., and ERIKSON, KAI. "The Confirmation of the Delinquent," *Chicago Review*, Winter 1957, Vol. 10, no. 4. Also in *The Condition of Modern Man in Society*, ed. Hendrik M. Ruitenbeek. New York: G. P. Putnam's Sons, 1962.

FEIFEL, HERMAN (ed.). *The Meaning of Death*. New York: McGraw-Hill Book Co., 1959.

———. "Death—Relevant Variable in Psychology," in *Existential Psychology*, ed. Rollo May. New York: Random House, 1961.

FEINSTEIN, OTTO. "Is There a Student Movement?" *New University Thought*, Summer 1961, Vol. I, no. 4, pp. 23-29.

FELDMAN, GENE, and GARTENBERG, MAX (eds.). *The Beat Generation and The Angry Young Men*. London: Souvenir Press, 1959.

FINGARETTE, HERBERT. *The Self in Transformation*. New York: Basic Books, 1963.

FRANKL, VIKTOR E. *The Doctor and the Soul*. New York: Alfred A. Knopf, 1955.

FREUD, SIGMUND. *Civilization and its Discontents*. New York: Doubleday Anchor, 1958.

———. *The Future of an Illusion*. New York: Doubleday Anchor, 1957.

———. *Group Psychology and the Analysis of the Ego*. New York: Bantam Books, 1960.

———. *Beyond the Pleasure Principle*. New York: Bantam Books, 1959.

———. *Collected Papers*. Vol. IV. London: Hogarth, 1956.

FRIEDAN, BETTY. *The Feminine Mystique*. New York: W. W. Norton and Co., 1963.

FRIEDENBERG, EDGAR Z. *The Vanishing Adolescent*. Boston: Beacon Press, 1960.

FROMM, ERICH, *Escape from Freedom*. New York: Rinehart, Holt & Winston, 1941.

———. *The Sane Society*. New York: Rinehart, Holt & Winston, 1955.

———. "Individual and Social Origins of Neurosis," in *Personality in Nature, Society, and Culture*, ed. Clyde Kluckhohn *et al*. New York: Alfred A. Knopf, 1959, pp. 515-521.

FROMM-REICHMANN, FRIEDA. *Principles of Intensive Psychotherapy*. Chicago: University of Chicago Press, 1950.

———. "Remarks on the Philosophy of Mental Disorders," *Psychiatry*, Vol. IX, 1946, pp. 293-308.

———. "Psychiatric Aspects of Anxiety," in *Identity and Anxiety*, ed. Maurice Stein *et al*. New York: The Free Press of Glencoe, 1960, pp. 129-144.

FROMM-REICHMANN, FRIEDA, AND MORENO, J. L. (eds.). *Progress in Psychotherapy*. New York: Grune and Stratton, 1956.

GALBRAITH, JOHN KENNETH. *The Affluent Society*. Boston: Houghton Mifflin, 1958.

GOFFMAN, ERVING. *The Presentation of Self in Everyday Life*. New York: Doubleday Anchor, 1959.

GOODMAN, PAUL. *Growing Up Absurd*. New York: Random House, 1960.

———. "Utopian Thinking," *Commentary*, July 1961, pp. 19-26.

HALL, EDWARD T. *The Silent Language*. New York: Doubleday & Co., 1959.

HEDERER, EDGAR. *Das Deutche Gedicht*. Frankfurt: Fischer-Bücherei, 1957.

HEIDEGGER, MARTIN, *An Introduction to Metaphysics*. New York: Doubleday Anchor, 1961.

———. *Existence and Being*. Chicago: Henry Regnery, 1949.

———. *Essays in Metaphysics*. New York: Wisdom Library, 1960.

———. *Sein und Zeit*. Tübingen: Neomarius Verlag, 1949.

———. *Was ist Metaphysik?* Frankfurt: Klostermann, 1949.

———. *Holzwege*. Frankfurt: Klostermann, 1950.

HESS, ROBERT D., and HANDEL, GERALD. *Family Worlds, A Psychosocial Approach to Family Life*. Chicago: University of Chicago Press, 1959.

Hölderlin. His Poems, tr. Michael Hamburger. London: Havrill, 1942.

HOOK, SYDNEY (ed.). *Psychoanalysis, Scientific Method, and Philosophy*. New York: New York University Press, 1959.

HORNEY, KAREN. *The Neurotic Personality of Our Time*. New York: W. W. Norton & Co., 1937.

HUIZINGA, JOHAN. *The Waning of the Middle Ages*. New York: Doubleday Anchor, 1956.

JASPERS, KARL. *Man in the Modern Age*. New York: Doubleday Anchor, 1957.

———. *Reason and Existenz*. New York: Noonday, 1955.

———. *Way to Wisdom*. New Haven: Yale University Press, 1960.

———. *Existentialism and Humanism*. New York: R. F. Moore, 1952.

———. *Philosophie*. Berlin: Julius Springer, 1932.

———. *Von der Wahrheit*. Munich: Piper, 1947.

———. *Der philosophische Glaube*. Munich: Piper, 1948.

KAFKA, FRANZ. *The Trial*. New York: Alfred A. Knopf, 1955.

———. *The Castle*. New York: Alfred A. Knopf, 1956.

———. *Selected Stories*. New York: Modern Library, 1952.

———. *The Penal Colony. Stories*. New York: Schocken Books, 1961.

KAHLER, ERICH. *The Tower and The Abyss*. New York: George Braziller, 1957.

KARDINER, ABRAM. *The Psychological Frontiers of Society*. New York: Columbia University Press, 1945.

KARDINER, ABRAM, and PREBLE, EDWARD. *They Studied Man*. New York: World Publishing Co., 1961.

KAZIN, ALFRED. "The Language of Pundits," *The Atlantic*, July 1961, pp. 73-78.

KENISTON, KENNETH. "Alienation and the Decline of Utopia," *The American Scholar*, Spring 1960. Also in *The Condition of Man in Modern Society*, ed. Hendrik M. Ruitenbeek. New York: G. P. Putnam's Sons, 1962.

KIERKEGAARD, SÖREN. *Fear and Trembling—The Sickness unto Death*. New York: Doubleday Anchor, 1954.

———. *Either/Or*. Vols. I, II. New York: Doubleday Anchor, 1959.

KINSEY, ALFRED C., et al. *Sexual Behavior in the Human Male*. Philadelphia: W. B. Saunders Co., 1948.

KLEIN, MELANIE. *The Psychoanalysis of Children*. New York: Evergreen Books, 1960.

KLUCKHOHN, CLYDE. *Mirror for Man*. New York: Premier Books, 1957.

———. et al. *Personality in Nature, Society, and Culture*. New York: Alfred A. Knopf, 1959.

LAING, R. D. *The Divided Self*. Chicago: Quadrangle Books, 1960.

LANDHEER, BART. *Pause for Transition*. The Hague: Martinus Nijhoff, 1957.

LARRABEE, ERIC. *The Self-Conscious Society*. New York: Doubleday & Co., 1960.

LARRABEE, ERIC, and MEYERSOHN, ROLF (eds.). *Mass Leisure*. New York: The Free Press of Glencoe, 1958.

LINDNER, ROBERT M. *Rebel Without A Cause*. New York: Evergreen Books, 1956.

———. *Prescription for Rebellion*. New York: Rinehart, 1952.

LINTON, RALPH. *The Study of Man*. New York: Appleton-Century-Crofts, 1936.

LOWRIE, WALTER. *A Short Life of Kierkegaard*. New York: Doubleday Anchor, 1961.

LYND, HELEN MERRELL. *On Shame and the Search for Identity*. New York: Harcourt, Brace and World, 1958.

MAILER, NORMAN. "She Thought the Russians Was Coming," *Dissent*, Summer 1961, pp. 408-412.

MANNHEIM, KARL. *Ideology and Utopia*. New York: Harvest Books, n. d.

MARCUSE, HERBERT. *Eros and Civilization*. Boston: Beacon Press, 1955.

MARGOLIES, JOSEPH. "Juvenile Delinquents: The Latter-Day Knights," *The American Scholar*, Spring 1960, pp. 211-218.

MASSERMAN, JULES H., and MORENO, J. L. *Progress in Psychotherapy, Vol. II: Anxiety and Therapy*, New York: Grune & Stratton, 1957.

MAY, ROLLO. *The Meaning of Anxiety*. New York: The Ronald Press Company, 1950.

———. *Man's Search for Himself*. New York: W. W. Norton & Co., 1953.

———. (ed.) *Existential Psychology*. New York: Random House, 1961.

MAY, ROLLO, ELLENBERGER, H. F., and ANGEL, A. (eds.). *Existence: A New Dimension in Psychiatry and Psychology*. New York: Basic Books, 1958.

McIVER, JOYCE. *The Frog Pond*. New York: Braziller, 1961.

MEAD, MARGARET. *Male and Female*. New York: Mentor Books, 1955.

———. *Sex and Temperament in Three Primitive Societies*. New York: Mentor Books, 1950.

———. "Culture Change and Character Structure," *Social Structure*. New York: Oxford University Press, 1949, pp. 18-34. Also in *Identity and Anxiety*, pp. 88-98.

———. "The Implications of Culture Change for Personality Development," *American Journal of Orthopsychiatry,* Vol. XXVII, 1947, pp. 633-646.

———. "Social Change and Cultural Surrogates," in *Personality,* (ed.) Clyde Kluckhohn *et al.* New York: Alfred A. Knopf, 1959, pp. 651-662.

———. "Administrative Contributions to Democratic Character Formation at the Adolescent Level," in *Personality* (ed.) Clyde Kluckhohn *et al.* New York: Alfred A. Knopf, 1959, pp. 663-670.

MERTON, ROBERT K. *Social Theory and Social Structure.* New York: The Free Press of Glencoe, rev. ed., 1957.

MILLS, C. WRIGHT. *White Collar.* New York: Galaxy Books, 1956.

———. *The Power Elite.* New York: Galaxy Books, 1959.

———. *The Sociological Imagination.* New York: Evergreen Books, 1961.

MOUSTAKAS, CLARK E. *Loneliness.* Englewood Cliffs: Prentice-Hall. Spectrum Books, 1961.

MULLER, HERBERT J. *The Uses of the Past.* New York: Galaxy Books, 1957.

MUMFORD, LEWIS. *The City in History.* New York: Harcourt, Brace & World, 1961.

Nation, The, May 27, 1961, Special Issue, "Rebels with a Hundred Causes."

NELSON, BENJAMIN (ed.). *Freud and the 20th Century.* New York: Meridian Books, 1957.

OBERNDORF, C. P. *A History of Psychoanalysis in America.* New York: Grune & Stratton, 1953.

PAPPENHEIM, FRITZ, *The Alienation of Modern Man.* New York: Monthly Review Press, 1959.

POWER, EILEEN. *Medieval People.* New York: Doubleday Anchor, 1954.

RAVEN, SIMON. "Boys Will Be Boys," *Encounter,* November 1960, pp. 19-24.

RECHY, JOHN. *City of Night.* New York: Grove Press, 1963.

REINHARDT, KURT F. *The Existentialist Revolt.* New York: Frederick Ungar Publishing Co., 1960.

RICKOVER, H. G. *Education and Freedom.* New York: Dutton Everyman Paperback, 1960.

RIEFF, PHILIP. "The American Transference: From Calvin to Freud," *The Atlantic,* July 1961, pp. 105-107.

RIESMAN, DAVID. *The Lonely Crowd.* New Haven: Yale University Press, 1950.

———. *Individualism Reconsidered.* New York: The Free Press of Glencoe, 1954.

———. *Constraint and Variety in American Education.* New York: Doubleday Anchor, 1958.

———. "The Search for Challenge," *New University Thought,* Spring 1960, Vol. 1, no. 1.

———. "Where is the College Generation Headed?" *The Atlantic,* April 1961, pp. 39-45.

———. "The Influence of Student Culture and Faculty Values in the American College," Ch. II, *The Year Book of Education, 1959.* Also in *The Condition of Man in Modern Society* (ed.) Hendrik M. Ruitenbeek. New York: G. P. Putnam's Sons, 1962.

RILKE, RAINER MARIA. *Fifty Selected Poems.* With English translations by C. F. MacIntyre. Berkeley and Los Angeles: University of California Press, 1947. Paperback edition, 1958.

———. *Rilke Poems 1906-1926.* Translated by J. B. Leishman. London: Hogarth, 1938.

_____. *The Notebooks of Malte Laurids Brigge.* New York: Capricorn, 1958.

ROEDER, RALPH. *The Man of the Renaissance.* New York: Meridian Books, 1958.

ROSENBERG, BERNARD, and WHITE, DAVID MANNING (eds.). *Mass Culture.* New York: The Free Press of Glencoe, 1957.

RUITENBEEK, HENDRIK M. (ed.). *Psychoanalysis and Social Science.* New York: Dutton Everyman Paperback, 1962.

_____. *Psychoanalysis and Existential Philosophy.* New York: Dutton Everyman Paperback, 1962.

_____. *The Dilemma of Organizational Society.* New York: E. P. Dutton, 1963.

_____. *The Problem of Homosexuality in Modern Society.* New York: E. P. Dutton, 1963.

_____. *Varieties of Modern Social Theory.* New York: E. P. Dutton, 1963.

_____. *Psychoanalysis and Contemporary American Culture.* New York: Delta Books, 1964.

SAPIR, EDWARD. *Culture, Language and Personality.* Berkeley and Los Angeles: University of California Press, 1956.

SARTRE, JEAN-PAUL. *Being and Nothingness.* New York: Philosophical Library, 1956.

SCHAAR, JOHN H. *Escape from Authority: The Perspectives of Erich Fromm.* New York: Basic Books, 1961.

SEELEY, JOHN R. *Crestwood Heights.* New York: Basic Books, 1956.

_____. "The Americanization of the Unconscious," in *The Atlantic,* July 1961, pp. 68-72. Also in *Psychoanalysis and Social Science,* ed. Hendrik M. Ruitenbeek, New York: Dutton Everyman Paperback, 1962.

SLOCHOWER, HARRY. "The Juvenile Delinquent and the Mythic Hero," *Dissent,* Summer 1961, pp. 413-418.

SOLOMON, BARBARA PROBST. "The Person Alone," *Dissent,* Summer 1961, pp. 404-407.

SPOTNITZ, HYMAN. *The Couch and The Circle: A Story of Group Psychotherapy.* New York: Alfred A. Knopf, 1961.

STEARN, JESS. *The Sixth Man.* New York: Doubleday & Co., 1961.

STEIN, MAURICE R. *The Eclipse of Community.* Princeton: Princeton University Press, 1960.

STEIN, MAURICE R., VIDICH, ARTHUR, and WHITE, DAVID MANNING (eds.). *Identity and Anxiety.* New York: The Free Press of Glencoe, 1960.

STEIN, MORRIS I. (ed.). *Contemporary Psychotherapies.* New York: The Free Press of Glencoe, 1961.

STERN, ALFRED, *Sartre: His Philosophy and Psychoanalysis.* New York: Liberal Arts Press, 1953.

STOODLEY, BARTLETT H. *The Concepts of Sigmund Freud.* New York: The Free Press of Glencoe, 1959.

STRAUSS, ANSELM. *Mirrors and Masks: The Search for Identity.* New York: The Free Press of Glencoe, 1959.

SULLIVAN, HARRY STACK. *The Interpersonal Theory of Psychiatry.* New York: W. W. Norton & Co., 1953.

_____. "The Theory of Anxiety and the Nature of Psychotherapy," *Psychiatry,* XII, 1949, pp. 3-12.

TAWNEY, R. H. *Religion and the Rise of Capitalism.* New York: Mentor Books, 1958.

TAYLOR, HENRY OSBORN. The Medieval Mind. London: The Macmillan Co., Vols. I, II. 1938.

TILLICH, PAUL. *The Protestant Era.* Chicago: University of Chicago Press, 1948.

————. *The Courage to Be.* New Haven: Yale University Press, 1952.

————. *Theology of Culture.* New York: Oxford University Press, 1959.

TOCQUEVILLE, ALEXIS DE. *Democracy in America.* New York: Vintage Books, two volumes, 1960.

TOPITSCH, ERNST. "The Sociology of Existentialism," *Partisan Review*, May-June 1954, Vol. XXI, no. 3, pp. 289-304.

TYVEL, T. R. "The Teddy Boy International: Unhappy Hooligans," *Encounter*, August 1961, pp. 17-31.

USSHER, ARLAND. *Journey Through Dread: A Study of Kierkegaard, Heidegger, Sartre.* London: Darwen Finlayson, 1955.

VAN DEN HAAG, ERNST (and RALPH ROSS). *The Fabric of Society.* New York: Harcourt, Brace and World, 1957.

————. "Psychoanalysis and Its Discontents," in *Psychoanalysis, Scientific Method, and Philosophy*, ed. Sydney Hook. New York: New York University Press, 1959.

————. "Of Happiness and of Despair We Have No Measure," in *Mass Culture.* (Rosenberg, Bernard, and White, David Manning, eds.). New York: The Free Press of Glencoe, 1957.

————. "Notes on New York Housing," in *Dissent*, Summer 1961, pp. 277-281.

WAUGH, EVELYN. *The Loved One.* New York: Dell Publishing Co., Inc., 1961.

WEBER, MAX. *The Protestant Ethic and the Spirit of Capitalism.* New York: Charles Scribner's Sons, 1958.

WEIGERT, EDITH. "Existentialism and Its Relation to Psychotherapy," *Psychiatry*, 1949, Vol. 12, pp. 399-412.

WEIL, SIMONE. *The Need for Roots.* Boston: Beacon Press, 1955.

WHEELIS, ALLEN. *The Quest for Identity.* New York: W. W. Norton & Co., 1958.

WHITE, LEONARD D. (ed.). *The State of the Social Sciences.* Chicago: University of Chicago Press, 1956.

WHYTE, WILLIAM H., JR. *The Organization Man.* New York: Doubleday Anchor, 1957.

————. "Individualism in Suburbia," *Confluence*, Vol. 3, no. 3, Sept. 1954.

WILSON, COLIN, *The Origins of the Sexual Impulse.* New York: G. P. Putnam's Sons, 1963.

WINNICOTT, D. W. "The Capacity to Be Alone," *Int. J. Psycho-Anal.*, 39, p. 416, 1958.

WITZLEBEN, HENRY D. VON. "On Loneliness," *Psychiatry*, Vol. 21, no. 1, February 1958, pp. 37-43.

WOLFF, KURT H. *The Sociology of Georg Simmel.* New York: The Free Press of Glencoe, 1950.

WOLSTEIN, BENJAMIN. *Irrational Despair.* New York: The Free Press of Glencoe, 1962.

WOOD, MARGARET MARY. *Paths of Loneliness.* New York: Columbia University Press, 1953; paperback, 1960.

Other MENTOR Books of Interest

☐ **PSYCHOANALYSIS AND PERSONALITY by Joseph Nuttin.**
The noted Belgian psychologist discusses the relation
between modern depth psychology and Christian philosophy. Newly revised edition.   (#MT426—75¢)

☐ **THE BOOK OF THE IT by Georg Groddeck.** An early
classic of psychoanalysis by a friend and contemporary
of Freud. With an Introduction by Ashley Montagu.
                                          (#MT352—75¢)

☐ **GESTALT PSYCHOLOGY by Wolfgang Kohler.** A classic
statement of the basic concepts of a psychological
theory which has profoundly influenced the progress and
direction of modern psychology.   (#MT644—75¢)

☐ **PHILOSOPHICAL SKETCHES by Susanne K. Langer.** A
noted philosopher discusses the relationship between
the human mind and the emotions.   (#MP567—60¢)

☐ **PHILOSOPHY IN A NEW KEY by Susanne K. Langer.** A
study of the symbolism of reason, rite and art, in clear,
readable style.   (#MT635—75¢)

☐ **PSYCHOLOGY OF SEX by Havelock Ellis.** Carl Van Doren
calls this volume "the best one-volume treatment of sex
in the English language."   (#MQ808—95¢)

☐ **HEREDITY, RACE AND SOCIETY (newly revised) by L. C.
Dunn and Th. Dobzhansky.** A fascinating study of group
differences: how they arise, the influences of heredity
and environment, and the prospects of race improve-
ment.   (#MP532—60¢)

**THE NEW AMERICAN LIBRARY, INC., P.O. Box 1478, Church Street
Station, New York, New York 10008**

Please send me the MENTOR BOOKS I have checked above. I am
enclosing $————————(check or money order—no currency
or C.O.D.'s). Please include the list price plus 10¢ a copy to cover
mailing costs. (New York City residents add 5% Sales Tax. Other
New York State residents add 2% plus any local sales or use taxes.)

Name————————————————————————

Address—————————————————————————

City————————————State————Zip Code————
Allow 2 to 3 weeks for delivery

p³⁰

SIGNET Books You Will Enjoy

☐ **AN ANALYSIS OF HUMAN SEXUAL RESPONSE edited by Ruth & Edward Brecher.** A complete explanation for the layman of the controversial Masters-Johnson research on sexual response. Includes commentary by leaders in the study of sexual behavior, as well as prominent social critics. (#T3038—75¢)

☐ **MAN'S SEARCH FOR HIMSELF by Dr. Rollo May.** An eminent psychologist explains how the individual may achieve self-fulfillment and conquer the insecurities of our troubled age by coming to terms with his own nature. "Highly recommended."—**Library Journal.**

(#Q3226—95¢)

☐ **UNDERSTANDING MEDIA by Marshall McLuhan.** A provocative, widely debated theory about how television and other present-day mass media are changing the cultural patterns of American life. (#Q3039—95¢)

☐ **THE INNER WORLD OF CHILDHOOD by Frances G. Wickes.** A new, revised edition of a classic study of child psychology which has won international acclaim. "It merits the serious attention of everybody who has anything to do with children . . ."—Carl Jung.

(#Q3499—95¢)

☐ **COMPLETE SEXUAL FULFILLMENT by Barbara Bross & Jay Gilbey.** In a revolutionary guide to sexual fulfillment in the light of today's changing morality, two experts in the field discuss all facets of the sexual relationship, sweeping away the long-standing clichés and replacing them with practical suggestions designed to add vigor and gratification to any sexual relationship.

(#Q3253—95¢)

THE NEW AMERICAN LIBRARY, INC., P.O. Box 1478, Church Street Station, New York, New York 10008

Please send me the SIGNET BOOKS I have checked above. I am enclosing $_____(check or money order—no currency or C.O.D.'s). Please include the list price plus 10¢ a copy to cover mailing costs. (New York City residents add 5% Sales Tax. Other New York State residents add 2% plus any local sales or use taxes.)

Name_____

Address_____

City_____State_____Zip Code_____
Allow 2 to 3 weeks for delivery